THE REFERENCE SHELF

Vol. 25   No. 3

REPRESENTATIVE AMERICAN SPEECHES: 1952-1953

Edited, and with introductions,
by
A. CRAIG BAIRD
Department of Speech, State University of Iowa

THE H. W. WILSON COMPANY
NEW YORK   1953

PREFATORY NOTE

REPRESENTATIVE AMERICAN SPEECHES: 1952-53 is the sixteenth in this annual series. Each volume contains some twenty "representative" speeches delivered by Americans, or others temporarily identified with this country. These sixteen volumes contain some 350 addresses by some 240 orators.

The speeches have been grouped according to subject matter classification. International Relations, Political Campaign Issues, National Ideals, Congressional Legislation, Educational Policies and Ideals, Management and Labor Problems, and Moral and Religious Attitudes and Questions illustrate such areas.

Students of public speaking may prefer an alternate classification, based upon speech occasions, such as farewell (Truman), acceptance (Stevenson), dinner meetings, radio and television (Nixon, Bonnell), political campaigns (Eisenhower, Stevenson, and others), judicial occasions, commencement convocations (Kirk), professional gatherings (Ford), Senate debates (Lehman, Holland), United Nations meetings (Lodge), inaugurations (Eisenhower), labor conventions, and pulpit (Winston, Bonnell).

This editor, as he has stated previously, disavows that these examples are the "best" of the year. No satisfactory method of voting has been devised to register decisively the "best" of the gigantic heap of oral productions during a twelve-month period just closing. At best it would be necessary to select the top "best" of a given speaking type (*e.g.*, MacArthur is near the top among *military* speakers).

The Introduction to each of the sixteen volumes deals with some phase of speech standards. Recent Introductions have treated the speaker's thought (1948-49), language (1949-50), delivery (1950-51), effectiveness in legislative and political speaking (1951-52). The present Introduction, besides summarizing the events of the period and their impact on speaking, adds a unit of comment on speech types.

The brief introduction to each speech touches on the background and gives some reaction to ideas, forms of support, organization, language, audience adaptation, delivery, and immediate outcome. The student is thus encouraged to explore much further these concepts in each speech.

The biographical notes in the Appendix invite further investigation of the speaker's background and career. As a starting point, the various *Who's Who's* and *Current Biography* are recommended.

The Table of Contents of each volume and the Cumulative Author Index are further aids to a systematic review of speakers and issues since 1937. Students are invited to classify the speakers there recorded. Thus a fairly representative list of important speakers of recent decades (this list grouped as legislative, sermonic, forensic, etc.), can be assembled.

These volumes are a highly efficient reference source, both for subject entries and for the light they throw on trends and problems and attitudes of our national life, 1936-53. Students of public address, extempore speaking, oral and written composition, the history and criticism of American public address, and students of social sciences and history will find this volume (and previous ones) a useful source book and learning stimulus.

The editor again acknowledges his gratitude to the various speakers, publishers, and others who have provided texts, and who have given permission for the reprints. Specific acknowledgment is made in each case.

Most of all, this editor is grateful to his students, graduate and undergraduate, whose progress in learning and whose sympathetic understanding of American civilization have been a continual inspiration to him.

April 20, 1953

A. CRAIG BAIRD

CONTENTS

PAGE

INTRODUCTION

ISSUES AND SPEAKERS OF 1952

Speechmaking is closely related to the social background of the times and to the immediate events. Factors of time and place affect heavily both the content and composition of the speech.

You are advised to project yourself into the scene itself that embodies a speech; to visualize the forces that influenced the speaker and that controlled the audience as of that moment.

What were the dominant issues and movements of 1952 and early 1953 that explain or largely explain what was talked about and how the talking was developed?

INTERNATIONAL PROBLEMS

Korea

The supreme issue of foreign policy, as far as Americans were concerned, was, how could we end that Korean slaughter of Americans and our allies? And how end the enormous financial drain and the destruction of material? The "sitzkrieg" with its steady depletion of our resources and of our military personnel caused mounting indignation in this nation. MacArthur's return and his speeches of 1951 further stirred general demand for results. Hopes for early solution soared during the presidential campaign. But despite the endless speechmaking of politicians, radio commentators, and other professionals, the question remained unresolved in April 1953. General Omar Bradley, for example, in March of this year, posed the choices, none of them apparently very practicable: (1) withdrawal from Korea; (2) hanging on to the 38th Parallel indefinitely; or (3) bombarding Manchurian bases, blockading China, and using atomic weapons. Thus the dilemma continued until the death of Stalin, the assumption of leadership by Malenkov, the exchange of sick and wounded prisoners in Korea, and the renewal of armistice negotiations. [1]

Western Europe

The main question of our foreign policy, nevertheless, continued to be that of Western Europe. Could Western Europe be sufficiently consolidated to defend itself against Soviet onslaught? Would the six nations comprising the European Defense Community ratify their military treaty? Would France work in harness with a revived Germany? Or was the tardiness of these countries a case again of "too little and too late"? The new Secretary of State, John Foster Dulles, visited the capitals of these nations and upon his return reported to Americans the dubious state of developments. Thus through State Department and other utterances the debate persisted in 1952-1953 as it had during the preceding year: how should Europe defend itself against Russia? And with the new peace offensive of Malenkov, would these nations be lulled into false security? [2]

United Nations, the Soviets, and "Peace"

Another aspect of this global issue of our relations with Russia was the fate of the United Nations and the proposals for "peace." During 1952-1953, as in the preceding years, the United Nations had been largely a sounding board for Soviet propaganda—without perceptible progress otherwise. Henry Cabot Lodge, Jr., the new Eisenhower-appointed ambassador to that body, immediately exchanged verbal blows with the Russians. [3]

The death of Stalin and the ascendancy of Malenkov apparently had altered not a whit the tension. Was the latest Russian "peace" offensive merely the same old propaganda line? Could the Russians be persuaded to signal for a truce in Korea and the mitigation of their pressures in West Germany and elsewhere?

---

[1] See Omar Bradley's speech at Miami, Florida, March 2, 1953, and President Dwight Eisenhower's address, at Washington, D.C., April 16, 1953. The succeeding references are to speeches in this volume.

[2] John Foster Dulles, February 12, 1953.

[3] Henry Cabot Lodge, Jr., February 25, 1953.

On the Senate floor also the issue was debated. Senator William Knowland, of California, on March 16, 1953, demanded that Russia be labeled "an aggressor." Senator John S. Cooper, of Kentucky, argued otherwise. The three differing Senate camps continued their argument, fundamentally the same attitudes that had dominated Senate debates on foreign policy since 1945: (1) isolationism (e.g., the 1953 position of Styles Bridges and his fellows); (2) the out-and-out Roosevelt-Truman position (e.g., that of Alexander Wiley, John Cooper); and (3) the intermediate position of nationalism combined with militant support of our allies and decisive action in the Far East and elsewhere (e.g., Senator Knowland).

The Demand for Knowledge

Other speechmakers criticized those in power for their alleged failure to inform the American public concerning the real situation. Senator Stuart Symington charged that we were preferring "butter" to "guns," and that it might be a case of our tragic lateness in military preparedness. He demanded that the American people should be given the facts of Russia's power and of our weaknesses.[4]

DOMESTIC PROBLEMS

Presidential Campaigns

Political speaking dominated the domestic scene of 1952. During the early months the primary campaigns enlisted many speakers; convention debating and oratory stirred the national audiences; and the Eisenhower-Stevenson campaign itself made issues other than that of Republicans vs. Democrats secondary.

The drawn-out primary campaigns moved on with vigor but with unusual acrimony. Harold Stassen, Robert Taft, Estes Kefauver, Richard Russell, W. Averill Harriman, Earl Warren, Robert Kerr, Douglas MacArthur, Alben Barkley, and at the last minute Dwight Eisenhower, were all entered or pushed into the lists.

[4] Stuart Symington, March 11, 1953.

The nominating conventions, at Chicago, had their usual color, their parades within the hall, and their clamor. Apparently no conventions during the previous twenty years had produced such sharp debating and deep disagreements. Each party obviously had within its own ranks those who held widely different political philosophies. The Republicans fought over the seating of delegates.[5] The Democrats were concerned with states' rights planks in their platform and with pledges for party solidarity in their campaign itself. Wide varieties of speech-making were used—debates in the committee sessions; party arguments on the floor concerning procedure, the seating of delegates, ratification of platforms; ceremonial addresses;[6] nominating speeches, and, at the close, impressive acceptance addresses.[7] Republican convention speakers included MacArthur, Hoover, Dirksen; among the Democrats addressing their convention were Truman and Eleanor Roosevelt.

The campaign speaking itself was as extensive and in some respects as acrimonious as almost any of these campaigns since 1884. Each candidate traveled and spoke endlessly. He talked by any means at his disposal—by radio, TV, rear platform, or in precinct halls, or at Madison Square Garden. Eisenhower, obviously no routine political speaker, improved through the weeks. His wartime reputation and personality counted heavily in his favor. Stevenson, however, became the speaker of the year—and foremost among political speakers of the past half century—with his wit, eloquence, philosophical overtones, and compositional originality.[8]

TELEVISION AND THE CAMPAIGN

How much did television change campaigning and what part did it play in the 1952 vote? For the first time in national politics, this new medium had been fully applied. The two parties spent directly some seven or eight millions on radio-TV and in-

---

[5] Donald Eastvold, July 9, 1952.

[6] Alben W. Barkley, July 23, 1952.

[7] Adlai Stevenson, July 26, 1952.

[8] Dwight Eisenhower, October 24, 1952; Adlai Stevenson, October 14, 1952.

directly the networks themselves and other sponsors contributed the equivalent of many more millions.

Television enabled Adlai Stevenson, comparatively unknown until he was drafted, quickly to make himself known to millions as a leader of power. Television, to cite another example, enabled Richard Nixon, overnight, through his skillful television techniques, to vindicate in the eyes of the voters his political honesty.[9]

Television, furthermore, brought the conventions to almost every American—although critics proved that the public exposure to endless hours of vapid oratory "unquestionably drove the viewers away in droves." These same critics, however, agreed that in general television tended to compel the candidates to focus more sharply on the issues, to minimize old-time political oratory, to help the voter to know "personally" each candidate, to increase public interest in national problems and the stand of each party, and to give each voter a first-hand insight into the political machinery behind the voting processes.[10]

New Regime

The year of speechmaking also marked the end of the Roosevelt-Truman regime and the restoration of Republicanism. The passing of the principles and programs of those twenty years evoked nostalgic speechmaking from the White House and wherever Democrats gathered. Notable was President Harry S. Truman's final broadcast, his "farewell to the nation." [11]

The inauguration ceremonies and Eisenhower's address began what many believed was to be a governmental philosophy sharply different from the so-called "socialistic" temper of the New Deal.[12]

[9] Richard Nixon, September 23, 1952.

[10] For detailed analysis of the political speaking, see Baird, A. Craig and collaborators, "Political Speaking in 1952: A Symposium," in *Quarterly Journal of Speech*, 38:265-99, October 1952; Haberman, Frederick and others, "The Election of 1952: A Symposium," *Quarterly Journal of Speech*, 38:397-414, December 1952.

[11] Harry S. Truman, January 15, 1953.

[12] Dwight D. Eisenhower, January 20, 1953.

AMERICAN IDEALS AND INDIVIDUAL RIGHTS

The issue of communism and national security continued with unabated intensity. The *cause célèbre* of Alger Hiss vs. Whittaker Chambers helped to dramatize the problem. It became a campaign issue. The question was whether the government was permeated with Communists and whether assaults on the character of citizens, before they had recourse to legal defense, was to be condoned; whether Senator Josph McCarthy and his investigative tactics were undermining American constitutional freedom and practices. The movement reflected itself in attempts by states to require oaths of teachers; attempts to purify textbooks; the banning of books and magazines; the endless investigations of loyalty; the endless questions as to security; the increased efforts to examine FBI files and to conduct the investigations over television with inference of guilt by association. These matters were hotly debated. Occasionally a statesmanlike address clarified the issue. Said Judge Learned Hand, "The mutual confidence on which all else depends can be maintained only by an open mind and a brave reliance upon free discussion." [13]

Affected by the changing economic philosophy accompanying the resurgence of Republicanism, many industrialists and theorists discussed the problem of economic controls. The question was pretty much settled by the Eighty-third Congress, first session, with its abandonment of most controls. A kindred issue, of rising significance as Britain, France, Western Germany, and Japan made their economic plight clear to this country, was that of "trade vs. aid." Henry Ford II was spokesman for many a speaker in his thoughtful analysis of the problem at a Chicago meeting.[14]

Labor continued its deliberations in conventions and before congressional committees that were interested in revising the Taft-Hartley Law. The American Federation of Labor mourned the passing of William Green. The Congress of Industrial Organizations also memorialized the death of Philip Murray.

[13] Learned Hand, October 24, 1952.
[14] Henry Ford II, February 17, 1953; Robert R. Young, February 17, 1953.

Also hotly contested in the United States Senate, accompanied by an alleged "filibuster" by some twenty senators, was the off-shore oil bill.[15]

Preachers and other moral leaders continued to ask, have American character and ideals deteriorated? Are Americans losing their sense of moral and ethical responsibility? [16]

Finally, the educators continued to concern themselves with the direction and character of education. What should be the character of the school and college curriculum? Of general education? The future of the humanities? The service of education to the state? [17]

Thus by radio and television, in Congress, in churches, at business and professional conferences, among college students, in villages, on farms, in mills and business centers, in homes and clubs, wherever people talked, these events were analyzed and argued, and in some cases translated into action.

SPEECH TYPES

The speeches in this volume may be classified according to the occasion. Many of them, obviously, might be placed in more than one category. Suggestive classifications would be as follows:

Congressional Speeches: Herbert H. Lehman's and Spessard Holland's "Tidelands Oil."

Executive Speeches: John Foster Dulles' "Western European Army"; Henry Cabot Lodge, Jr.'s "Russian Support of Korean Aggression"; Stuart Symington's "The Truth Makes Us Free."

Political Campaign Speeches: Adlai Stevenson's "America's Role"; Dwight D. Eisenhower's "Crusade for Peace."

Political Convention Speeches: Donald Eastvold's "For Seating Eisenhower Delegates"; Alben W. Barkley's "The People's Crusade."

Acceptance Speeches: Adlai Stevenson's "Acceptance Speech."

[15] Herbert H. Lehman and Spessard L. Holland, April 13, 1953.

[16] John Sutherland Bonnell, January 4, 1953; Alexander Winston, March 17, 1953.

[17] Grayson Kirk, June 5, 1952; Monroe Deutsch, January 6, 1953.

Inaugural Speeches: Dwight D. Eisenhower's "Inaugural Address."

Dinner Speeches: Monroe Deutsch's "The Foes of the Humanities."

Professional Lectures: Learned Hand's "The Preparation of Citizens for Their Political Duties"; Henry Ford II's "The Free World Can't Trade on a One-Way Street."

Forums: Robert R. Young's "A Marriage of Business and Education."

Commencement Addresses: Grayson Kirk's "Historical Perspective and Current Issues."

Radio and TV Addresses: Richard Nixon's "Apologia"; John Sutherland Bonnell's "Making Life Worth Living."

Sermonic Occasions: John Sutherland Bonnell's "Making Life Worth Living"; Alexander Winston's "There Lies Our Frontier."

Speeches of Farewell: Harry S. Truman's "Farewell to the Nation."

Reports by Military Leaders: Omar Bradley's "Four Courses of Action in Korea."

FOREIGN RELATIONS

WESTERN EUROPEAN ARMY [1]

JOHN FOSTER DULLES [2]

John Foster Dulles, Secretary of State, addressed the nation on the evening of February 12, 1953, on the problem of the development of a Western European army. The speech was given over the combined radio and television networks.

Mr. Dulles had just returned from a ten-day tour of seven European capitals—Rome, Paris, London, Bonn, The Hague, Brussels, and Luxembourg. It was his first overseas trip since his appointment as Secretary.

The speech had the typical problem-and-solution construction. The issue was clearly stated (shall a "fire trap be rebuilt?") The development included a résumé of the pertinent events of the past twelve months, an analysis of the critical situation now facing the allies, a conciliatory reference to what had been done, a refutation of the argument (advanced by the Soviet propaganda machine and echoed by many Western European political leaders) that the United States was not to be trusted with such responsibilities; and a solution (quick rearming by our allies and the cooperation of the United States, the latter governed by a "sober and restrained policy"). Dulles, by implication, assured his listeners that we would not engulf the nations in a third world war (i.e., we would not do so by our Korean-Chinese moves). His speech was also designed to inform his American public of the facts, and to remind us again of the size of our stake and of our grave and great responsibilities.

In the light of what Dulles was trying to do in enlisting approval from and securing action by Western Europe, and in quickening Americans to their role of responsibility, the persuasion of this speech deserved sound analysis by students of speech and history.

The speaker's delivery here was businesslike and brusque, without Churchillian eloquence and with a minimum of nuance in voice technique.[3]

I returned this week from a trip to Europe in company with Mr. Stassen, the Director of our Mutual Security Agency.

[1] Text supplied by the Department of State.
[2] For biographical note, see Appendix.
[3] For further comment on Dulles as speaker, see, for example, his "The Japanese Peace Treaty," in *Representative American Speeches: 1951-52*, p41-7.

We have reported to the President; I have met, and shall meet further, with congressional leaders. Now I wish to report to you.

You may wonder why, with so much to do at home, we went so quickly abroad. The reason was the tremendous importance to the United States of real unity in Europe and the fact that it seemed that some of our European friends might be changing their minds about moving to this goal.

The problem in simple terms is this:

Europe is made up of people who possess an essential unity. They have given a clear and special meaning to the concept of Western civilization. Yet Europe has remained politically divided. This has led to recurrent wars, which have involved us. It has so weakened the Western European countries that today no one of them could offer strong resistance to the Red armies.

This situation both distresses and endangers us. Europe is the cradle of our civilization, and its industrial power could cruelly hurt us if it were controlled by our enemies.

It has been clear for some time that the biggest single post-war task would be to end the disunity in Europe which makes for weakness and war.

As the Second World War blazed up, I wrote "Continental Europe has been the world's greatest fire hazard. The whole structure is now consumed in flames. When the time comes to rebuild, we should not reproduce a demonstrated fire-trap."

Today we and the free peoples of Europe are all face to face with that very problem. Shall a demonstrated fire-trap be rebuilt? Or cannot the wit of man devise something better?

When the first program of interim aid to Europe was before the Senate in 1947, I urged, before the Foreign Relations Committee, that in granting European aid "the basic idea should be, not the rebuilding of the prewar Europe, but the building of a new Europe, which, more unified, will be a better Europe." That point of view was emphatically adopted by Congress. It was written into the policy declaration of the Marshall Plan act and into our military assistance acts, and that concept underlay the implementation of the North Atlantic Treaty Organization and the stationing of United States troops in Europe. None of these measures was looked upon as in itself adequate to defend Europe. But these steps, together with the creation of a unified continental Europe, would produce a strength which could deter aggression.

These are the ideas that enlightened European leaders themselves put forth. We have not been trying to impress an American scheme on Europe but to support the plans of the European leaders themselves.

They have already done much. As an outstanding example, they have created, under what is called the Schuman Plan, a single political authority to deal with the coal and iron resources of Germany, France, and the adjacent states. Last Sunday Mr. Stassen and I saw that authority first go into practical operation at its capital at Luxembourg.

Our European friends also tackled the vital problem of military unity. Last May the six continental countries of France, Germany, Italy, Belgium, the Netherlands, and Luxembourg signed a treaty to create a European Defense Community. Under that treaty each of the six countries would give up having a separate national army on the Continent and would join in building there a single European army. It was contemplated that the treaties could be promptly ratified, so that the plan could be made operative in six months.

We in the United States were delighted that our European friends had taken this bold step toward making Europe strong and vigorous in its own right. However, the six months from last May went by without any effective steps to ratify, and the six months has now been prolonged to nine months. This has been somewhat disconcerting to us, because the plans for our own security are based on the assumption that the North Atlantic Treaty Organization, which does not include Germany, would be bolstered by the European Defense Community, which would draw on German military strength to create a solid continental European military establishment.

During the past seven years we have contributed about thirty billion dollars to Europe. We have tens of thousands of our armed forces in Europe. We have made the effort because the security of Europe vitally affects our own security. But our effort will not permanently serve Europe or ourselves or humanity unless it fits into a constructive program for European unity. Nothing that the United States can do will ever be enough to make Europe safe if it is divided into rival national camps.

President Eisenhower himself said recently that he was impressed with the "feebleness" of alternatives to the European Defense Community.

It was to discuss all of these problems that President Eisenhower asked Mr. Stassen and me to go to Europe. We went to seven European capitals—first Rome, then Paris, then London, then Bonn, then The Hague, then Brussels, and then Luxembourg. Our conclusion was that the project for a European Defense Community was not dead but only sleeping. We did not get any concrete promises or pledges from our European friends, and we did not give any. We did come back with the feeling that there is a good chance that the European Defense Community will be brought into being. There are plenty of hurdles to be overcome. But we believe that there is a will to proceed. We hope that in the coming weeks this determination will be translated into concrete evidence that real progress is being made. Without that, future planning will be difficult. Candor requires us to say this.

NATO is now a far-flung organization. It includes not only countries in this hemisphere but in the North Atlantic and in the Mediterranean. But the core of this far-flung structure is the six continental countries of Western Europe, which have made the European Defense Community treaty. Unless their military and economic strength is to be combined, as this treaty contemplates, the whole NATO organization has a fatal weakness. The European Defense Community is needed to give the North Atlantic Treaty Organization a stout and dependable heart.

I do not pretend that it is easy to accomplish this. National habits of thought and traditions have grown strong. The countries concerned have often in recent years been enemies. They have fought each other, and there are proud memories of victories and the bitter memories of defeat. This means that greatness is needed if unity is to be achieved. That quality, however, is not lacking. We saw it in fact in the peoples of Europe as they had to face the physical disaster of the recent floods. We also found among the statesmen of Western Europe, and so far as we could judge among the peoples of Western Europe, a real determination to take the hard political decisions which would bury the evil of the past and fortify the good.

After our friendly talks, we know, and gladly report, that the political leaders in each of these countries are men of vision and stature. They look not backward but forward. They see the land of promise that lies ahead and they desire to move into it.

Having spent most of my time in talking about what we hope the European countries will do, I would like to conclude with a mention of what the governments and peoples of Europe expect of us.

Our friends in Western Europe, knew, when General Eisenhower was with them in Europe, how deep and firm was his interest in European unity—political, economic, and military. On this trip we were able to assure them that President Eisenhower continues to hold the same interest, the same conviction, with regard to European unity.

In each of these seven countries we visited we found good will and friendliness on the part of the governments and most of the people, but we also found some fear that the United States is not qualified to give the free world the kind of leadership which it needs at this critical moment. It is conceded that we have the material power, but it is questioned whether we have the accumulated wisdom to make the best use of that power. They are particularly concerned because they now have to deal with a new Republican administration, after having worked for twenty years in war and peace with a Democrat administration. To them, as to many Americans, a Republican administration is a novelty, and the unknown always carries a certain amount of fear.

The talks which we had with the political leaders of the countries we visited went far, I think, to dispel these fears insofar as official quarters are concerned. However, the public and the opposition parties seize upon incidents and upon statements made here which seem to them to be reckless. Unscrupulous persons use such incidents and statements as reasons why the European nations should not trust us.

It is important for us all to remember that we do carry a tremendous responsibility. Any false step could mean disaster not only for us but for our friends. Possibly our friends would suffer even more than we ourselves. Therefore, we must be sober and restrained in our national conduct.

That does not mean being timid and afraid to take the initiative, to speak frankly or to make hard decisions. Indecision, weakness, and vacillation are the qualities which most often lead to war. It does mean that in order to win and hold the confidence of those whom we need as friends and allies, we must at all times play the part of a nation which is fully aware of the grave responsibility which it carries.

That is the kind of leadership we shall get from President Eisenhower, who is accustomed to carry heavy responsibilities and calmly make grave decisions. We shall do well to follow the example which he will set. At this dangerous time peace and security depend upon clear vision, righteous purpose, and firm performance. Let us all work together to achieve these goals.

FOUR COURSES OF ACTION IN KOREA [4]

OMAR N. BRADLEY [5]

General-of-the-Army Omar N. Bradley, then Chairman of the Joint Chiefs of Staff, gave this address at the Palm Beach Round Table, Palm Beach, Florida, on Monday, March 2, 1953.

His question was, What program shall the United States adopt to end the Korean war? A basic issue of the campaign, the American people in early 1953 continued to agitate the problem and to look to the Eisenhower leadership for early solution.

General Bradley, obviously interested in informing the general public concerning the military possibilities in Korea, introduced the problem with unusual wariness. He needed to remove audience inhibitions regarding military leadership; to recall his listeners both to the ideals of peace and yet to the practical difficulties that barred the way. During the week of February 14 he had briefed the members of the Senate Foreign Relations Committee and on February 19 had done so to Eisenhower and to almost a hundred congressmen. His introduction, a relatively long one, aimed to conciliate, reassure, and to further establish audience confidence in his own motives and good judgment.

His four chief and seven ancillary military steps as "ways out" were largely to stimulate genuine facing of the facts, thinking and action. The speaker was interested in creating sound public opinion, free from emotional explosiveness. For example, he reminded his public that we were not yet in a third world war—even though some Washington leaders were so proclaiming. Bradley's speech was a plea for frank observation of the situation, accompanied by patience and caution in our every move. As such it was a good sample of persuasiveness.

The General's delivery is unimpressive. His voice is somewhat high and tight. He is no MacArthur. But the prestige of his effective military leadership and the deep sincerity of his long series of public utterances have given him deserved rating as a military platform spokesman. [6]

What I have to say now about Korea is only my personal opinion, and from a strictly military viewpoint. In broad per-

[4] Text and permission for this reprint furnished by the Department of Defense, Office of Public Information. Because of the length of this speech, only a section is here included.

[5] For biographical note, see Appendix.

[6] For further comment on General Bradley, see "Long Range Military Policy," in *Representative American Speeches: 1949-50*, p66-74.

spective, I believe that the United Nations have four courses of military action open to us in Korea.

One course of action—but one which I believe the American people and their allies would not condone—would be to withdraw our forces and get out of Korea. This would greatly jeopardize the authority of the United Nations. And all of our allies would begin to lose confidence. Furthermore, our great efforts and sacrifice would appear to have been in vain. Finally, communism in Asia would have a free rein and the tyranny which accompanies communism—already so vividly painted in blood in China—would spread like a plague across all of Asia to include our friends in Southeast Asia and India and Pakistan.

Second, we could continue the present pressure in Korea, keeping our casualties to a minimum, and causing the greatest casualties to the enemy that we could inflict.

The third course of military action open to the United Nations is of greater scope than the second: We could continue the present pressure in Korea, causing the greatest casualties possible to the enemy; and we could take the additional military steps, from time to time, where a military advantage might accrue. We would hope that the Communist Chinese, because of increasing pressure, would get tired and eventually quit. But even some of these additional measures in Korea might require high-level international decisions, for all of them are not entirely within the present scope of military authority.

The fourth course of action is a big step beyond the third: It involves taking any one, or any combination, of military steps open to us *in order to get a decision in Korea* even while we realize that it might eventually involve us in an all-out war with Communist China. We must realize that broadening the war in this way might pin down the bulk of our military power on the continent of Asia, and could eventually develop into World War III.

We would have to assess the risk with each step taken. We would have to be prepared for the counter-measures the Communists could take and the counter-measures that eventually the Soviet Union might take because of the Sino-Russian treaty.

Preliminary to this course of action, it would seem to me that the United Nations, and especially the United States, would have to make long-term foreign policy decisions on future relations in the Far East.

The additional military steps referred to in the many discussions of these third and fourth courses of action are divided into many possibilities: Some could be taken alone, or several could be taken in combination. You have undoubtedly read about some of them in your newspapers and have heard many of them discussed in public:

1. By adding to our forces in Korea—which would call for a much greater mobilization of men and industry—and taking the necessary casualties, United Nations forces could drive to the Yalu River and free Korea of the Communist Chinese.

2. We could extend the air war into Manchuria. This would require bombardment of the Communist air bases across the Yalu and would have to include the devastation of the communications centers and military targets in the manufacturing centers of Manchuria, if it were to be effective.

3. The United Nations could intensify the economic sanctions. Everyone realizes that some strategic materials are still being delivered to the enemy.

4. To augment this the United Nations could declare a naval blockade. This course of action is complicated by the status of the British colony Hong Kong. Naval experts tell us that to be most effective this action would have to include the blockade of two Chinese ports now under control of the Soviet Union: Dairen and Port Arthur, and the blockade of coastal shipping.

5. Another course of action—which could advance our line to the narrow waist of Korea—would be a combined ground, air and navy offensive.

6. We could also continue the improvement and enlargement of the Republic of Korea forces so that fewer American divisions are in the line. We have already started on this, and only the economic and manpower limitations involved set a practical limit on this course of action.

7. Another factor which could be added to the war if a practical opportunity should present itself is the use of atomic weapons.

All of these possibilities—and many others—have been studied and considered in the past and are constantly being considered as ways and means of reaching a decision for the United Nations in Korea. Many of them have not been taken in the past because we didn't have the power to do them effectively; many of them were not taken—and are not taken now—because a military advantage does not accrue. Many of these actions could only be taken if the larger, high-level policy decisions were made. . . .

RUSSIAN SUPPORT OF KOREAN AGGRESSION [7]

HENRY CABOT LODGE, JR. [8]

Henry Cabot Lodge, Jr., gave this speech before the Political and Security Committee of the United Nations, on February 25, 1953, as the opening speaker of the current session of the General Assembly of the United Nations. The address, Lodge's first before that group after his appointment by President Eisenhower as United States Ambassador, had little rating as an oratorical document. An address to so many nations obviously called for simple, unadorned and clearcut phrasing. But the talk had great significance in the drive to consolidate United Nations opinion against the Soviets.

The persuasive speech was well organized, compactly developed. It turned out to be a redeclaration of United Nations principles with respect to armistice and peace terms for Korea.

The Lodge argument had immense propagandistic potentialities. It affirmed the continuation under Eisenhower of the same United States support of our military commitments in Korea; our supreme goal of peace; our adherence to the Indian resolution for solving that conflict; Russia's obvious support of a continued war there—to be carried on "to the last Chinese"—and Russia's ability to end that war at any time; our platform of equal treatment of all human beings; our condemnation of the persecution of Christians, Jews, Moslems; our policy of promoting freedom from want; our denunciation of dictators and our faith in popular control; and the United States policy of nonformulation of new proposals for a Korean armistice.

Lodge's citation of ten facts proving Russia's direct hand in the Korean war and his general pattern of argument and appeal were designed to take the propaganda offensive and to force the Soviets into a defensive role.

On March 2, Soviet Foreign Minister Andrei Vishinsky, in a six-thousand-word speech, admitted the Lodge accusations that the Soviets had supplied the Chinese Reds with war supplies and other help, but reiterated the charge that the United States had started that war and that the Republican leaders did not want peace. The death of Stalin on March 5 obscured for the time the United Nations debate over the Korean issue. [9]

[7] The text was supplied by the office of Henry Cabot Lodge, Jr., United Nations, New York City.

[8] For biographical note, see Appendix.

[9] For further comment on Lodge as speaker before the United Nations Assembly, see his "Stop Being Afraid," in *Representative American Speeches: 1950-51*, p37-43.

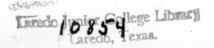

To appear before this gathering of statesmen from all over the world as the representative of my country is a unique distinction. It is an honor to be associated here with all of you—an honor of memorable significance to me.

Since the last meeting of the General Assembly, there has been a change in the government of the United States—a change in which the losers have neither been disgraced—nor, I may say, liquidated.

The American people wish to establish a lasting peace and regard the United Nations as a vital means to that end. As President Eisenhower said: "Respecting the United Nations as the living sign of all peoples' hope for peace, we shall strive to make it not merely an eloquent symbol, but an effective force. And in our quest for an honorable peace, we shall never compromise, nor tire, nor ever cease."

Every element of American life is eager for peace. For the sake of peace we have put up our resources; we have sent our men. Even the most fanatic critics of the United States are unable to point a finger at any group having the slightest weight or importance in America which does not believe in peace.

This love of peace exists in all Americans regardless of party. It was for that reason that my predecessors at the last Assembly voted for the Indian resolution—a resolution which spared no effort to meet the issues; which declared unequivocally for peace; which was passed by a vote of the General Assembly which was overwhelming. If ever an action represented the conscience of the world and the striving of suffering humanity for peace it was the passage of that resolution.

It seemed impossible that there could be rulers in this world who would object to this offer, but it soon appeared that there were. The regimes of China and of North Korea have turned it down, and, of course, when they did it, they must have known that they were telling the world in effect: "We wish to continue the bloody struggle in Korea; and, therefore, tell you that you can only solve the Korean problem on our terms." We, who are determined to end the war on a just basis, must all note this development with regret and seek the reasons for it.

Therefore, we should first ponder the statement of Mr. Chou En-lai, the Foreign Minister of the Chinese Communist regime, who in his political report of February 4, 1953, spoke of the Korean war and said that it "has greatly"—and I quote—"reinforced the strength and influence of the world camp of peace and democracy headed by the Soviet Union"—an unwittingly candid admission, by the way, as to the identity of those whose word he heeds.

Mr. President, for many generations Americans have had close relations with China and have learned to esteem the wisdom of the Chinese people. We realize that there are genuinely democratic forces at work throughout the world, which have been suppressed in some areas including China. These forces reflect the human desire for a richer, freer life. Forces of this same kind built our own country.

There is no doubt that some Chinese believed the promise of progress which was made to them by their present rulers. Such promises are always attractive. But being an intelligent people with a long tradition of wisdom they certainly cannot approve of the present situation in which young manhood of China is being slaughtered in response to a policy which appears to be admittedly dictated from Moscow.

Apparently, the Soviet Union, with its own special brand of magnanimity and generosity, is determined to carry on the war to the last Chinese.

Mr. Chou En-lai's description of the Korean war as a positive good to communism shocks us. We repudiate it. We are sure the Chinese people would repudiate it if they were free to do so.

This brings me naturally to another somber truth. This is: that the Soviet Union is actively assisting the aggressors in Korea on a scale which makes possible the continuance of that aggression and determines its scope. The following facts therefore, should be placed clearly and frankly before world opinion.

Here are ten facts which the world should face:

Fact Number One is that Soviet planning instigated the original aggression, which was subsequently maintained by Soviet training and equipment, notably Soviet aircraft, Soviet artillery, Soviet T-34 tanks, and Soviet automatic weapons.

Fact Number Two is that the North Korean forces which were virtually destroyed after the Inchon landing in the fall of 1950 fled across the Yalu River, behind the screen of the Chinese Communists who were then entering Korea. They reappeared on the battlefront in late winter reconstituted, reorganized, and almost completely equipped with weapons of Soviet manufacture.

Fact Number Three is that the flow of Soviet equipment is constant and steady, and accounts for the increase of combat effectiveness of the enemy over the past year.

Fact Number Four is that the Chinese Communists who entered the fighting with normal light equipment are now fighting with heavy equipment, supplied by the Soviet Union.

Fact Number Five is that naval mines in large number, which have been picked up or washed ashore off the Korean coast have been mines of Soviet manufacture.

Fact Number Six is that the planes which the United Nations Command has been encountering over North Korea have been MIG-15's and other aircraft, manufactured, and supplied by the Soviet Union.

Fact Number Seven is that recently United Nations forces have encountered a new type of Soviet plane, the IL-28, which is now a part of the air forces of the Communist aggressors over North Korea.

Fact Number Eight is that in spite of heavy losses, the Chinese Communist and North Korean air forces have grown until they today have some 2500 aircraft of which half are jets, all manufactured and supplied by the Soviet Union.

Fact Number Nine is that the Soviet Union provides the replacements for these aircraft which United Nations forces shoot down over North Korea. Our experts estimate that the Soviet Union has contributed in excess of 4400 planes to fight against the United Nations in Korea.

Fact Number Ten is that the anti-aircraft guns in North Korea, including many which are radar-controlled, are of Soviet origin.

The Soviet representatives are hereby challenged to disprove these facts. They show how far the Soviet Union has gone to broaden the war—how, since the fall of 1950, the United Nations has not been fighting a local enemy, but the vast manpower resources of Communist China supported by the material resources of the entire Soviet world.

And then, Mr. President, there are people who have the crudity to come here and make sanctimonious speeches about world peace.

The whole world knows the truth: that except for the active aid furnished to the North Korean and Chinese Communist aggressors by the Soviet Union, the war in Korea would now be over. Like the ostrich who sticks his head in the sand and thinks that no one sees him, the rulers of the Soviet Union are so bemused by their own propaganda that they do not recognize the extent to which world opinion holds them responsible for aiding and abetting this great crime against the peace of the world.

The rulers of the Soviet Union can stop the war whenever they want to—and Mr. Vishinsky knows it.

Mr. President, peace not only depends on collective security; it must also be based on equal treatment of human beings. As long as there is racial or religious discrimination, just so long is the day of peace postponed. Conditions are not perfect in any country in this regard but in many lands—I know this is true in my own—great and successful advances are being made.

We have, however, observed with indignation the persecution of Christians, Moslems, and Jews that has been taking place in the Soviet Union for some time. That discrimination is not only wicked; it will also in the end prove to be totally ineffective because there is an undefeatable quality in human nature which will always resist totalitarian attempts to destroy religious and ethnic freedom.

Mr. President, I conclude.

To build peace there must, of course, be collective security.

To build peace there must be equal treatment of people without discrimination as to race, creed or color.

To build peace there must also be freedom from the specter of want. There is no use in talking to a starving man about freedom or democracy. We stand ready to work for peace along all these lines too.

Finally, we believe that peace, like every other great human problem, is best solved by governments which are controlled by the people, in which public officials are the servants of the people —countries in which the word "dictatorship" is a bad word, and not countries in which officials proudly boast of dictatorship and give it the misleading title of "Dictatorship of the Proletariat."

We believe that the counsel of many men of good will produces more collective wisdom than that of a few. We believe in the people; we have faith in the people. We believe the people are competent to make their own decisions, and that a man is not rendered all-wise by being made all-powerful.

Mr. President, the facts I have just presented concerning the words of the Chinese Communists and the actions of the Soviet Union are a monstrous answer to the adoption by this Assembly of the Indian resolution. For these reasons there is little point in reformulating at this session the principles on which that resolution was based. The Indian resolution, in the words of a great American on another occasion, raises a standard to which the wise and honest can repair. When the day comes that the aggressors in the Far East have a change of heart—for whatever reasons; and they can be many—it will not be difficult for them to show it. Failure to end the fighting in Korea is not due to any lack of cleverness with words here in the United Nations. It is due to the frankly announced desire of the Communists to continue the war.

Mr. President, I reserve my right to speak further on the Korean item at a later point in the debate.

A PEACE PROGRAM [10]

Dwight D. Eisenhower [11]

President Dwight D. Eisenhower gave this address at a luncheon of the American Society of Newspaper Editors, in Washington, on Thursday, April 16, 1953.

The speech was generally hailed as a significant and conclusive statement of American foreign policy at a critical time in America's decision as to a proper road to follow in dealing with the new regime in Soviet Russia.

Premier Georgi Malenkov and his colleagues Vyacheslav Molotov and Lavrenti Beria had, since the burial of Joseph Stalin on March 9, apparently launched upon a much more conciliatory policy toward the Western nations.

As the President spoke, disabled prisoners of war in Korea were in process of being exchanged. Further negotiations for an armistice were about to be resumed. The New York stock exchange had sharply declined on the assumption of coming peace. But the basic problems that had sharply separated the Soviets from the United Nations remained, in Korea, Indo-China, Japan, Germany, and elsewhere around the globe.

The American public, as well as the many nations that supported our general point of view, called for an affirmative statement from Washington that would embody our general approach to these apparent Soviet gestures toward peace. Eisenhower's speech was the answer to such call.

The President's address is to be studied in its character as a constructive propaganda document. It sounded our notions of how to get peace; held out to all nations the benefits of channeling war expenditures into peaceful currents—for education and general usefulness; played up the obvious results of disarmament; assured all nations of their right to determine their own form of government; and challenged Russia to take a cooperative stand concerning the great differences that at present blocked peace. Eisenhower's appeal, nevertheless, was accompanied by his implication that the alternative was an atomic war. (The experimental atomic bomb explosions that continued on the Yucca Flat proving grounds in Nevada reinforced his implications.)

Both political parties immediately endorsed the speech. The American press strongly approved it. The Western European press likewise

[10] Text as recorded by the New York *Times*. The speech as recorded in the *Congressional Record*, 99:3317-3319, April 16, 1953, begins with the statement, "In this spring of 1953."

[11] For biographical note, see Appendix.

was enthusiastic. Prime Minister Winston Churchill, on April 17, called the Eisenhower peace plan "massive and magnificent," and pledged Britain's support.

All in all it was the most striking address thus far given by the new President.

President Bryan, Distinguished Guests of this Association and Ladies and Gentlemen:

I am happy to be here.

I say this and I mean it very sincerely for a number of reasons. Not the least of these is the number of friends I am honored to count among you.

Over the years we have seen, talked, agreed and argued with one another on a vast variety of subjects under circumstances no less varied. We have met at home and in distant lands. We have been together at times when war seemed endless, at times when peace seemed near, at times when peace seemed to have eluded us again.

We have met in times of battle, both military and electoral, and all these occasions mean to me memories of enduring friendship.

I am happy to be here for another reason.

This occasion calls for my first formal address to the American people since assuming the office of the presidency just twelve weeks ago. It is fitting, I think, that I speak to you, the editors of America.

You are in such a vital way both representatives of and responsible to the people of our country. In great part upon you, upon your intelligence, your integrity, your devotion to the ideals of freedom and justice themselves depend the understanding and the knowledge with which our people must meet the fact of twentieth century life.

Without such understanding and knowledge they would be incapable of promoting justice; without them they would be incapable of defending freedom.

Finally, I am happy to be here at this time before this audience because I must speak of that issue that comes first of all in the hearts and minds of all of us—that issue which most urgently challenges and summons the wisdom and the courage of our whole people.

This issue is peace.

In this spring of 1953 the free world weighs one question above all others: The chance for a just peace—just peace—for all peoples.

To weigh this chance is to summon instantly to mind another recent moment of great decision. It came with that yet more hopeful spring of 1945, bright with the promise of victory and of freedom. The hope of all just men in that moment, too, was a just and lasting peace.

The eight years that have passed have seen that hope waver, grow dim, and almost die. And the shadow of fear again has darkly lengthened across the world.

Today the hope of free men remains stubborn and brave, but it is sternly disciplined by experience.

It shuns not only all crude counsel of despair, but also the self-deceit of easy illusion.

It weighs the chance for peace with sure, clear knowledge of what happened to the vain hope of 1945.

In the spring of victory the soldiers of the Western Allies met the soldiers of Russia in the center of Europe. They were triumphant comrades in arms. Their peoples shared the joyous prospect of building, in honor of their dead, the only fitting monument—an age of just peace.

All these war-weary peoples shared, too, this concrete, decent purpose: To guard vigilantly against the domination ever again of any part of the world by a single, unbridled aggressive power.

This common purpose lasted an instant—and perished. The nations of the world divided to follow two distinct roads.

The United States and our valued friends, the other free nations, chose one road.

The leaders of the Soviet Union chose another.

The way chosen by the United States was plainly marked by a few clear precepts which govern its conduct in world affairs.

FIRST: No people on earth can be held—as a people—to be an enemy, for all humanity shares the common hunger for peace and fellowship and justice.

SECOND: No nation's security and well-being can be lastingly achieved in isolation, but only in effective cooperation with fellow-nations.

THIRD: Any nation's right to a form of government and an economic system of its own choosing is inalienable.

FOURTH: Any nation's attempt to dictate to other nations their form of government is indefensible.

AND FIFTH: A nation's hope of lasting peace cannot be firmly based upon any race in armaments, but rather upon just relations and honest understanding with all other nations.

In the light of these principles, the citizens of the United States defined the way they proposed to follow, through the aftermath of war, toward true peace.

This way was faithful to the spirit that inspired the United Nations: To prohibit strife, to relieve tensions, to banish fears. This way was to control and to reduce armaments.

This way was to allow all nations to devote their energies and resources to the great and good tasks of healing the war's wounds, of clothing and feeding and housing the needy, of perfecting a just political life, of enjoying the fruits of their own toil.

The Soviet Government held a vastly different vision of the future.

In the world of its design, security was to be found—not in mutual trust and mutual aid—but in force: Huge armies, subversion, rule of neighbor nations. The goal was power superiority—at all cost. Security was to be sought by denying it to all others.

The result has been tragic for the world and for the Soviet Union it has also been ironic.

The amassing of Soviet power alerted free nations to a new danger of aggression. It compelled them in self-defense to spend unprecedented money and energy for armaments. It forced them to develop weapons of war now capable of inflicting instant and terrible punishment upon any aggressor.

It instilled in the free nations—and let none doubt this—the unshakable conviction that, as long as there persists a threat to freedom, they must, at any cost, remain armed, strong and ready for any risk of war.

It inspired them—and let none doubt this—to attain a unity of purpose and will beyond the power of propaganda or pressure to break now or ever.

There remained, however, one thing essentially unchanged and unaffected by Soviet conduct: This unchanged thing was the readiness of the free world to welcome sincerely any genuine evidence of peaceful purpose enabling all peoples again to resume their common quest of just peace. And the free world still holds to that purpose.

The free nations, most solemnly and repeatedly, have assured the Soviet Union that their firm association has never had any aggressive purpose whatsoever.

Soviet leaders, however, have seemed to persuade themselves —or tried to persuade their people—otherwise.

And so it has come to pass that the Soviet Union itself has shared and suffered the very fears it has fostered in the rest of the world.

This has been the way of life forged by eight years of fear and force.

What can the world—or any nation in it—hope for if no turning is found on this dread road?

The worst to be feared and the best to be expected can be simply stated.

The worst is atomic war.

The best would be this: A life of perpetual fear and tension; a burden of arms draining the wealth and the labor of all peoples; a wasting of strength that defies the American system or the Soviet system or any system to achieve true abundance and happiness for the peoples of this earth.

Every gun that is made, every warship launched, every rocket fired signifies—in the final sense—a theft from those who hunger and are not fed, those who are cold and are not clothed.

This world in arms is not spending money alone.

It is spending the sweat of its laborers, the genius of its scientists, the hopes of its children.

The cost of one modern heavy bomber is this: A modern brick school in more than thirty cities.

It is: Two electric power plants, each serving a town of sixty thousand population.

It is: Two fine, fully equipped hospitals.

It is some fifty miles of concrete pavement.

We pay for a single fighter plane with a half-million bushels of wheat.

We pay for a single destroyer with new homes that could have housed more than eight thousand people.

This is—I repeat—the best way of life to be found on the road the world has been taking.

This is not a way of life at all, in any true sense. Under the cloud of threatening war, it is humanity hanging from a cross of iron.

These plain and cruel truths define the peril and point the hope that come with this spring of 1953.

This is one of those times in the affairs of nations when the gravest choices must be made—if there is to be a turning toward a just and lasting peace.

It is a moment that calls upon the governments of the world to speak their intentions with simplicity and with honesty.

It calls upon them to answer the question that stirs the hearts of all sane men: Is there no other way the world may live?

The world knows that an era ended with the death of Joseph Stalin. The extraordinary thirty-year span of his rule saw the Soviet empire expand to reach from the Baltic Sea to the Sea of Japan, finally to dominate 800,000,000 souls.

The Soviet system shaped by Stalin and his predecessors was born of one world war. It survived with stubborn and often amazing courage a second world war. It has lived to threaten a third.

Now a new leadership has assumed power in the Soviet Union. Its links to the past, however strong, cannot bind it completely. Its future is, in great part, its own to make.

This new leadership confronts a free world aroused, as rarely in its history, by the will to stay free.

The free world knows—out of the bitter wisdom of experience—that vigilance and sacrifice are the price of liberty.

It knows that the peace and defense of Western Europe imperatively demand the unity of purpose and action made possible by the North Atlantic Treaty Organization, embracing a European Defense Community.

It knows that Western Germany deserves to be a free and equal partner in this community; and that this, for Germany, [is] the only safe way to full, final unity.

It knows that aggressions in Korea and in Southeast Asia are threats to the whole free community to be met only through united action.

This is the kind of free world which the new Soviet leadership confronts. It is a world that demands and expects the fullest respect of its rights and interests. It is a world that will always accord the same respect to all others.

So the new Soviet leadership now has a precious opportunity to awaken, with the rest of the world, to the point of peril reached, and to help turn the tide of history.

Will it do this?

We do not yet know. Recent statements and gestures of Soviet leaders give some evidence that they may recognize this critical moment.

We welcome every honest act of peace.

We care nothing for mere rhetoric.

We care only for sincerity of peaceful purpose—attested by deeds. The opportunities for such deeds are many. The performance of a great number of them waits upon no complex protocol but only upon the simple will to do them.

Even a few such clear and specific acts—such as [the] Soviet Union's signature upon an Austrian treaty, or its release of thousands of prisoners still held from World War II—would be impressive signs of sincere intent. They would carry a power of persuasion not to be matched by any amount of oratory.

This we do know: A world that begins to witness the rebirth of trust among nations can find its way to peace that is neither partial nor punitive.

With all who will work in good faith toward such a peace, we are ready—with renewed resolve—to strive to redeem the near-lost hopes of our day.

The first great step along this way must be the conclusion of an honorable armistice in Korea.

This means the immediate cessation of hostilities and the prompt initiation of political discussions leading to the holding of free elections in a united Korea.

It should mean—no less importantly—an end to the direct and indirect attacks upon the security of Indo-China and Malaya. For any armistice in Korea that merely released aggressive armies to attack elsewhere would be a fraud.

We seek, throughout Asia as throughout the world, a peace that is true and total.

Out of this can grow a still wider task—the achieving of just political settlements for the other serious and specific issues between the free world and the Soviet Union.

None of these issues, great or small, is insoluble—given only the will to respect the rights of all nations.

Again we say: The United States is ready to assume its just part.

We have already done all within our power to speed conclusion of a treaty with Austria which will free that country from economic exploitation and from occupation by foreign troops.

We are ready not only to press forward with the present plans for closer unity of the nations of Western Europe but also, upon that foundation, to strive to foster a broader European community, conducive to the free movement of persons, of trade and of ideas.

This community would include a free and united Germany, with a government based upon free and secret ballot.

This free community and the full independence of the East European nations could mean the end of the present unnatural division of Europe.

As progress in all these areas strengthens world trust, we could proceed concurrently with the next great work—the reduction of the burden of armaments now weighing upon the world. To this end we would welcome and enter into the most solemn agreements. These could properly include:

1. The limitation, by absolute numbers or by an agreed international ratio, of the sizes of the military and security forces of all nations.

2. A commitment by all nations to set an agreed limit upon that proportion of total production of certain strategic materials to be devoted to military purposes.

3. International control of atomic energy to promote its use for peaceful purposes only, and to insure the prohibition of atomic weapons.

4. A limitation or prohibition of other categories of weapons of great destructiveness.

5. The enforcement of all these agreed limitations and prohibitions by adequate safeguards, including a practical system of inspection under the United Nations.

The details of such disarmament programs are manifestly critical and complex. Neither the United States nor any other nation can properly claim to possess a perfect, immutable formula. But the formula matters less than the faith—the good faith without which no formula can work justly and effectively.

The fruit of success in all these tasks would present the world with the greatest task—and the greatest opportunity—of all. It is this: The dedication of the energies, the resources, and the imaginations of all peaceful nations to a new kind of war. This would be a declared, total war, not upon any human enemy, but upon the brute forces of poverty and need.

The peace we seek, founded upon a decent trust and cooperative effort among nations, can be fortified—not by weapons of war—but by wheat and by cotton, by milk and by wool; by meat, timber and rice.

These are words that translate into every language on earth.

These are the needs that challenge this world in arms.

This idea of a just and peaceful world is not new or strange to us. It inspired the people of the United States to initiate the European Recovery Program in 1947. That program was prepared to treat, with equal concern, the needs of Eastern and Western Europe.

We are prepared to reaffirm, with the most concrete evidence, our readiness to help build a world in which all peoples can be productive and prosperous.

This government is ready to ask its people to join with all nations in devoting a substantial percentage of any savings achieved by real disarmament to a fund for world aid and reconstruction. The purposes of this great work would be: To help other peoples to develop the undeveloped areas of the world, to stimulate profitable and fair world trade, to assist all peoples to know the blessings of productive freedom.

The monuments of this new kind of war would be these: Roads and schools, hospitals and homes, food and health.

We are ready, in short, to dedicate our strength to serving the needs, rather than the fears, of the world.

I know of nothing I can add to make plainer the sincere purpose of the United States.

I know of no course, other than that marked by these and similar actions, that can be called the highway of peace.

I know of only one question upon which progress waits. It is this: What is the Soviet Union ready to do?

Whatever the answer be, let it be plainly spoken.

Again we say: The hunger for peace is too great, the hour in history too late, for any government to mock men's hopes with mere words and promises and gestures.

Is the new leadership of the Soviet Union prepared to use its decisive influence in the Communist world—including control of the flow of arms—to bring not merely an expedient truce in Korea but genuine peace in Asia?

Is it prepared to allow other nations, including those in Eastern Europe, the free choice of their own form of government?

Is it prepared to act in concert with others upon serious disarmament proposals?

If not—where then is the concrete evidence of the Soviet Union's concern for peace?

There is, before all peoples, a precious chance to turn the black tide of events.

If we failed to strive to seize this chance, the judgment of future ages will be harsh and just.

If we strive but fail, and the world remains armed against itself, it at least will need to be divided no longer in its clear knowledge of who has condemned humankind to this fate.

The purpose of the United States, in stating these proposals, is simple.

These proposals spring—without ulterior motive or political passion—from our calm conviction that the hunger for just peace is in the hearts of all peoples—those of Russia and of China no less than of our own country.

They confirm to our firm faith that God created men to enjoy, not destroy, the fruits of the earth and of their own toil.

They aspire to this: The lifting, from the backs and from the hearts of men, of their burden of arms and of fears, so that they may find before them a golden age of freedom and of peace.

Thank you.

THE TRUTH MAKES US FREE [12]

W. Stuart Symington [13]

Senator W. Stuart Symington (Democrat, Missouri) gave this address before a capacity audience at the closing session of the Seventh Annual Philadelphia Bulletin Forum, on the evening of March 11, 1953.

His thesis, clearly stated, was that the American people have not been properly informed concerning national defense; that if given such information they will give proper support to the program; and that the national Defense Department has been inefficient and should have a wholesale reorganization.

This speaker had much facility in speech composition here and in his other speeches. His argument was well knit, his logic set forth in popular terms easily grasped, and the emotional enforcement well timed and expressed. His sharp questions strongly enforced his main proposition and were designed to stimulate his national audience to seek concrete answers. His pessimistic refrain that "butter" had won out over "guns" and that Washington and public alike were unduly complacent was in line with his speeches of 1947-1950. Then, as Secretary of the Air Force, he had argued vigorously and without success for what he regarded as an adequate military defense program.

Although no orator, this senator in speaking voices conviction and incorporates ample logic and evidence. His audience adjustments and influence are unusually well marked.

This address came at the juncture of General James Van Fleet's report that United Nations forces in Korea had had insufficient ammunition. A few days later President Eisenhower had declared our national defense against atomic attack was woefully inadequate and that a budget of some sixteen billion should be allocated to protect this country.[14]

It is an honor to be here tonight. And it is fitting that I should talk about truth in great affairs as part of the Evening Bulletin Forum, a newspaper known for its devotion to the truth.

Truth is essential to the workings of a government such as ours, one that is based upon the consent of the governed.

---

[12] Text furnished through the courtesy of Senator Symington with permission for this reprinting.

[13] For biographical note, see Appendix.

[14] For further comment on Senator Symington and his speaking, see *Representative American Speeches: 1949-50*, p75-84.

"The reason of the law is the life of the law." That maxim is sound, because when a democratic people understand why things are asked of them, they respond fully as partners in a common enterprise, sharing its risks and its benefits.

No folk-saying was ever more fallacious than "what you don't know won't hurt you." Lack of knowledge does hurt you.

That lack, in our democracy, may be fatal to our survival.

We are a great people; and I believe we will do whatever may be required of us by the given situation. We will not flinch from the truth, however grim it may be.

But it is a sad fact that for a long time some of our national leaders—in both parties—have not told us the whole brutal truth about the world in which we live.

Whether this is because they mistakenly believe we are weaklings, or believe we are children who will cry if it appears we are about to lose some of our toys, I do not know.

But I do know this. The failure to tell us the truth has already injured us. The continuance of that failure may destroy us.

The face of the world was forever changed on a day in September 1949. That was the day the Soviet Union exploded the atomic bomb.

America then lost its monopoly of that weapon—and was thereupon faced with a peril it had never before known.

At that very time, however, we chose to further heavily decrease our armed strength.

Eight months later, in May 1950, our government announced that hopes for peace were better than at any time since World War II; and that therefore even less money would be required for defense the following year.

That was May. In June the Communists struck in Korea.

For a long time, both before and after the start of the Korean war, we followed the advice of those Pentagon people who glibly explained to the National Security Council why America could not afford adequate rearmament.

The Government accepted this price tag on security, rejecting the advice of a few congressional leaders and others who plead that a balanced budget would mean nothing if it resulted in a slave state.

Certain fiscal leaders, who should have been talking about fiscal affairs, suddenly became military experts; and advanced the cause of one type of jet engine over another.

Certain scientists, who should have stuck to science, desired to enter politics; so they wrote vague, misleading books on military strategy; and became so-called experts on the organization of the Department of Defense.

In other words, too many people were minding other people's business, to the detriment of sound decisions in their own areas of responsibility.

This led to confusion, and therefore compromise, and therefore military weakness.

When in the fall of 1950, however, the Kremlin gave the order for the Chinese to cross the Yalu, Stalin's intention to take high risks for world conquest finally became clear to everybody.

But even that did not bring us to our senses, although our armies were then being driven back in what was possibly the worst military reverse ever suffered by the United States.

The American people were still assured they could take it easy. We were told that we could handle this new Soviet aggression with one hand, while we piled the other hand high with butter and automobiles and television sets.

The results have not been pleasant. Only last week General Van Fleet told our Committee that his troops were short of ammunition while they attempted to resist the mass attacks of the Communist hordes! He said that every month during the twenty-two months he had been in Korea there had been a serious shortage of ammunition, which at times became critical. Our policy of "plenty of butter" could not appeal to those young Americans who were short of ammunition as they faced the enemy.

Now the Administration has changed. But one thing has not changed. The policy of butter and guns has not shifted in favor of guns. The balanced budget is still around the corner. But so also is the most dangerous enemy free men have ever known.

I do not believe this policy is right.

Nor would the American people believe it right if they knew the truth.

Some say we are spending on national defense as much as we can afford. But no cost is too high if it is necessary to maintain freedom.

Yet it is nonsensical to spend ourselves into bankruptcy because of a wastefully inefficient defense organization.

There is a saying in business that an organization can stand outside competition, but can't stand inside competition. A firm will ultimately fall apart when its executives are at cross purposes with one another.

The Department of Defense is suffering from inside competition and the American people are suffering because of it. If the Pentagon operated under a unification law which gave efficient business and military administration, with less service friction, we'd get far more defense for far less money.

The beginning of wisdom in great affairs is to take a hard look at your adversary. Then compare your strength with his.

At the time Columbus discovered America, Russia was a small country, in population and area. Now it controls 750 million people—about one third of the world population; and about one sixth of the earth's surface.

And remember this: within the past thirty years Russia has jumped from the oxcart into the airplane. Its own science is first-rate, and it has at its disposal superb German and satellite brains.

In communism it has an immensely effective weapon among the masses of people in countries with a low standard of living.

Its resources, in men and materials, are now colossal; and, as many of our own resources have dwindled through consumption, Russia's have increased through conquest.

Today the Kremlin's Chinese satellites, backed by Soviet pilots, tanks and planes, cross and recross the Yalu.

At the same time we provide them with a military university for the instruction of their technicians, at no loss to them except some equipment and a few pilots.

At very little cost to the Russians, we are teaching them how to defeat us if they decide to expand the Korean war into World War III.

Rather than coming up with the truth to the people, we follow the tragic steps of certain World War II allies, by again attempting to purchase a nervous neutrality. . . .

Talks of this character occasionally meet with some acceptance —plus the hope conditions will get better—but invariably the conviction remains that even if our failure to face reality results in another Pearl Harbor, we will never lose a war.

In this air atomic age, however, the opening battle may well decide the war.

Hitler announced his intentions to conquer the world. Because we would not believe him we had the catastrophic second world war.

Stalin announced the same intention. I believe him. We certainly cannot afford not to believe him.

Stalin is now dead. This is unlikely to affect the world favorably, because Communists believe fanatically that they must bring all men under their bloodstained banner.

In my opinion, they will not deviate from their purpose unless they are checkmated.

Fortunately for us, we do not stand alone against Soviet Russia. We have staunch allies. But America is the final bulwark of the free world. What we do, or fail to do, will determine the fate of all men everywhere. . . .

In summary, are we, the American people, satisfied with the way the international picture is shaping up? If not, what should we do?

The people must know what they ought to do.

In an effort to help with that decision, the Government should now publish answers to such questions as:

How many men under arms did the United States and its allies have at the end of World War II—and how many did the Soviets have?

How many men under arms do the United Nations have today—and how many is it estimated the Soviets have?

How many long-range submarines did the Germans and the Japanese have at the start of World War II? How close did that number, in 1942 and 1943, come to choking us off, by sea, from the rest of the world?

How many long-range submarines is it estimated the Soviets now have?

How many long-range bombers, capable of striking the United States, is it estimated the Soviets have today? How many long-range bombers, capable of striking Russia, has the United Nations?

How many jet bombers has the Soviet? How many has the United Nations?

How many modern jet fighters for defense against Russian atomic bombers has the United Nations? How many modern jet fighters is it estimated the Soviets have for defense against our retaliating bombers?

What is the 1952 estimate of modern Soviet jet fighter production? What is the estimate for 1953?

What are the comparable United Nations modern jet fighter production figures for 1952 and 1953?

What is the estimated comparable jet bomber production of Russia and the United Nations for the two years in question?

Aren't we supposed to match the Kremlin's quantity of manpower with our quality of horsepower instead of trading man for man with the Communist hordes? Therefore why don't we use the atomic bomb on military targets in North Korea?

Now we come to the three most important questions of all— the answers to which may well foretell whether or not we are to remain a free people. These questions are:

What is our Government's estimate of that date when the Soviets may have what they might consider enough atomic weapons to launch a successful attack, by air and submarine, against the United States?

Is our Defense Department properly organized for the most efficient utilization of the taxpayer's dollar in building a defense, against such an attack, by that date?

And is the size and form of our defense program aimed toward the maximum national defense possible against atomic attack by that date?

In other words, will we be ready when that critical day comes?

The answer in my opinion is No—and I believe the facts prove it.

In any case, why not give the facts to the people?

If that were done the people themselves would demand a wholesale reorganization of our Defense Department, so as to get more defense for less money.

This position is not to be construed as a criticism of the Administration. For years a few of us have tried to get the truth of our military position out to the people, because we believe our national security, far from preventing the publication of this information—rather demands it.

The answer to these questions is the only way all the people —not just a few in Washington—can make an intelligent assessment of the nation's forearmament program.

Once the truth is understood, Americans will accept any challenge, will make any sacrifice, to the end that they and their children can become strong—and therefore remain free.

PRESIDENTIAL CAMPAIGN OF 1952

FOR SEATING EISENHOWER DELEGATES [1]

DONALD EASTVOLD [2]

Mr. Donald Eastvold gave this argument in rebuttal on Wednesday evening, July 9, 1952, before the Republican National Convention meeting in the International Amphitheatre, Chicago.

The credentials committee, Taft-controlled, all during that day had heard the testimony concerning the seating of contested delegates from Georgia and Texas. The credentials committee recommended the seating of the Taft delegates. The issue was then transferred to the convention floor.

As soon as Rep. Ross Risley of Oklahoma had moved the acceptance of the committee ruling in favor of the pro-Taft group from Georgia, Eastvold proposed a counter-resolution supporting the Eisenhower delegates.

Eastvold's argument was methodically organized, limited to a specific issue, developed under thirteen points, and was presented with persuasive calmness. Its mood was more deliberative than epideictic. The speech was in sharp contrast to that of the succeeding debater, Senator Everett Dirksen, of Illinois. This senator, much more oratorical, developed the famous diversionary attack on Thomas Dewey: "We followed you before and you took us down the road to defeat."

Mr. Eastvold then presented the rebuttal speech here reprinted.

The convention floor vote on Georgia was 607 to 531 in support of the Eisenhower position. The Taft forces then conceded the Texas case. Undoubtedly, the three-day battle for seating the contested delegates profoundly affected the 1206 delegates and partly explains Eisenhower's nomination on the first ballot.

THE TEMPORARY CHAIRMAN: The argument in rebuttal for the Proponents of the Minority Report which has been brought to the convention as a substitute will now be commenced by Senator Eastvold, the delegate from the state of Washington. [*Applause*]

MR. EASTVOLD: Mr. Chairman, ladies and gentlemen of the convention, I am a young man from the state of Washington and I feel like I am in pretty high company tonight.

[1] Text furnished through the courtesy of the Republican National Committee.
[2] For biographical note, see Appendix.

After listening to the attorney-general of the state of Wisconsin, the Honorable United States Senator from the state of Illinois, I feel placed upon my shoulders a responsibility which I wonder whether I will be able to fulfill. [Applause]

However, ladies and gentlemen of this convention, I did not come here tonight to deal in personalities. [Applause]

Ladies and gentlemen of this convention, the National Committee and the Credentials Committee are not on trial but their decisions are on trial. [Applause]

And I want to report to you that two of the decisions of the National Committee have already been reversed in the Credentials Committee.

One of those decisions relates to the state of Louisiana and I believe only honor will remain with our Republican party for having taken that move.

I want to also report to you that there is one gentleman on our Credentials Committee who also serves in the capacity of the National Committeeman who heard the evidence twice and while he served on the National Committee in the same contest he voted one way as he heard it one way, and then when he sat on the Credentials Committee he heard it another, so that there is in the Republican party's national structure a difference between individuals and even in one individual's own mind. [Applause]

Now, ladies and gentlemen of the convention, there is an old adage in the law: Beware of the young attorney with a book. Ladies and gentlemen of the convention, I hope I can make that old adage a reality tonight.

I have with me a decision of the United States Supreme Court which deals with the general problem of which is the supreme body to decide questions involving political contests and the seating of the members of the political parties.

I will not presume tonight to read to you all of that decision but I would like to quote to you from the case of Colegrove vs. Green. . . . Remember now that this is the Supreme Court of the United States, not an inferior court, and I do not mean to infer by that that the court is inferior, but the Supreme Court of the United States says. . . :

Nothing is clearer than [that] this controversy concerns matters that bring the court into immediate and active relation to a party contest. From the determination of such issues this court has traditionally held aloof. It is hostile to a democratic system to involve the judiciary in the politics of the people.

Now, ladies and gentlemen of this convention, I think it might be interesting for about five minutes to talk about the facts and the law in the case of the state of Georgia.

I would like to call your attention to the fact, first of all, that the group which now enjoys a temporary seat in this convention, the Foster group, lays its sole claim to the legal title of the Republican party based on a decision of a trial court in its own state.

We have heard nothing in the National Committee, we heard nothing in the Credentials Committee, and we have heard nothing tonight about the contributions of that particular group in the state of Georgia during the last eight years. [*Applause*]

Now, I do not mean to infer, and I emphasize this with great sincerity, I do not mean to infer as some of our national magazines have inferred, that this particular court in the state of Georgia or any court in the state of Georgia is dishonest or fraudulent.

I am a young man that has a high regard for the courts in my native state of Washington and I share in that regard the respect for the courts of the sister states. However, I do say that there were some mighty irregular proceedings surrounding this case in the state of Georgia that you should know about.

There was a district delegate elected on April 26 and the suit wasn't brought in the court and filed until June 10, so that it couldn't be heard before June 30.

It seems to me, as we say in the law, that the party was a little tardy in instituting its action. At least it was a great imposition on the contesting party to have it set on June 30 in the trial court in Georgia and begin hearings before the National Committee in Chicago the next day.

VOICE FROM THE FLOOR: Do you say that that is a reflection on the court?

MR. EASTVOLD: No, but I am wondering what the motives were of the party instituting the action. Secondly, it is known to every lawyer in this room, and you know, too, those of you who are not lawyers, that you have to be served with a summons and complaint before you are legally responsible to respond in an action.

Eight of the twenty-five defendants in this action have not as yet been served as of this date and the case has been tried before the judge in a court of Georgia.

Clearly, ladies and gentlemen, we prize as one of our constitutional rights the trial by jury. In the state of Georgia when there is a question of fact in matters of this kind the parties are entitled to a trial by jury.

The people I represent demanded a trial by jury and were denied the same by the court. Ladies and gentlemen of the convention, even if these irregularities had not existed I would submit to you for your consideration that the Supreme Court in this case is the National Convention of the Republican party [*Applause*] and that the Supreme Court of the Republican party has passed on this question twice before; in 1944 it passed and determined in favor of the Tucker group; in 1948 the Supreme Court of the Republican party passed on this question and decided it in favor of the Tucker group. Are we forever going to be considering and retrying this case?

We have a proposition in the law known as *res adjudicata* which means that there must some time be an end to litigation. I submit that the end should have been in 1948. [*Applause*]

But lastly, their claim is based upon a court decision which if the court decision is read in its entirety it says this—one sentence, listen; this is a copy of the decision of the court: "This opinion has nothing to do with the delegates or officers of either platform." The court decision upon which they rely is not even authority for the proposition that their delegates should be seated in this convention. [*Applause*]

Now, ladies and gentlemen of this convention, we heard nothing as to the activities of the Foster group. Let me tell you in a few brief moments why the Tucker group should be seated.

First, it should be seated because of the hard work it has done faithfully in the vineyard of the Republican party. The Republican party vote in the state of Georgia under the leadership of the Tucker group has increased by 50 per cent in the past eight years. *[Applause]*

The Republican party under the recognized leadership of the Tucker group has faithfully made its regular contributions and met its quota financially to the National Committee.

In contradistinction to this, I asked, personally, before the Credentials Committee, the gentleman, the leader of the faction, whether his group has contributed anything to the financial status of the Republican party in the last eight years and he said No.

I submit to you that this group known as the Foster group goes into hiding after each National Convention and comes crawling out about six months before our party meets to nominate a president.

Secondly, I submit to you that the Tucker group should be seated because it has been the recognized Republican party in Georgia for the last eight years under the present leadership. It has been recognized by two National Conventions; it has been recognized by the National Committee which has seated this delegation, who has been a member of this committee, and has met with them through the past eight years.

Third, this party has been recognized because they received the official call of the Republican party. Even the Secretary of State in the state of Georgia recognized as of July 2 that the Tucker group was the official group, the official Republican party of Georgia, and he was aware of the decisions of his own trial court.

The Secretary of State of Georgia himself recognized that the Republican Party National Convention is the Supreme Court in the area of seating of delegates.

Even the leader of the Foster group, in a letter dated in 1948 which I have in my hand, addressed to Mr. Tucker, recognized him as the official leader of the party of Georgia.

Ladies and gentlemen of this convention, it would set the Republican party in Georgia back twenty years if we will stand for a policy of disorder, if we fail to reaffirm the decisions of this National Convention of 1944 and of 1948; we will sentence the Republican party in Georgia to a doom of confusion, disillusionment and defeat.

I urge you to support the substitute motion; I urge you to vote Aye when the roll is called. [*Applause.*]

THE PEOPLE'S CRUSADE [3]

ALBEN W. BARKLEY [4]

Vice President Barkley delivered this address before the Democratic National Convention, in the International Amphitheatre, Chicago, on the evening of July 23, 1952.

The Vice President had not long before the convening of his party announced his candidacy for the presidency. At the opening, on Monday, July 21, the CIO and AFL leaders had told Barkley that they could not support him because of his age.

Popular with all groups within his party, his withdrawal had merely increased the high respect and affection in which he was held. The convention greeted him with a spontaneous and prolonged demonstration. His extempore address, broadcast over radio and television, was rated as one of the two or three outstanding demonstrative addresses of the convention.

The personal arguments in this oration were strongly marked. The delivery was that of energetic "old-fashioned oratory," not well adapted to TV-radio. Mr. Barkley's impassioned rhetoric (with parallelism and balanced structure) was enlivened with humor. Old timers rated the performance as equal to that of Bryan and his "Cross of Gold" speech in 1896.

Barkley continued to be in great demand as lecturer as well as political speaker.[5]

Delegates and guests of this great convention: I have been a delegate at large from the state of Kentucky at every Democratic convention since 1920.

I am more firmly convinced of the righteousness of the Democratic cause tonight than I have ever been before in my entire life.

I wish first to express my profound thanks to the honorable Frank McKinney, chairman of the National Democratic Committee, for his generous invitation to me to address this convention at this hour. I am not here as a candidate for any office that this convention can confer.

Reprint here is from the New York *Times*, July 24, 1952.

[4] For biographical note, see Appendix.

[5] For further comment on Barkley and examples of his speaking, see *Representative American Speeches: 1938-39*, p53-9, "Foreign Policies of Roosevelt"; *1943-44*, p 188-99, "Against Roosevelt's Tax Veto"; *1948-49*, p96-100, "Tribute to Senator Barkley and Response."

If I were a candidate, I would not be here at this hour because I recognize the proprieties that ought to prevail among men who seek office. I am, therefore, in somewhat the situation of the country gentleman who for many years had gone to his county seat every Saturday in his farm wagon drawn by two mules.

On all of these occasions he came home intoxicated. He had a gentle pair of mules, they knew the way home, they drove the wagon home, drove up into the locked gate and stopped in front of the house. Each night the boys would go out and unhitch the team and take it to the barn and take the old gentleman in and put him to bed.

On one of these Saturday nights the boys unhitched the team, took it to the barn but left their father in the wagon-bed. As the sun came up over the horizon he aroused himself, rubbed his eyes and stood erect.

He went to the front of the wagon and looked out over the tongue and saw no mules. He went to the rear and looked out over the wagon's hind gate and saw no mules.

He went again to the front and looked over the mule-less tongue and then said to himself: "I either lost a damn good pair of mules, or I've found a damn good wagon."

Neither am I here tonight as the Vice President of the United States though I have the honor to hold that distinguished office. I am not here as a delegate from the state of Kentucky though I am a delegate from the state of Kentucky.

I am here tonight as an American talking to a great body of Americans representing a greater body of Americans interested in what we say or do in this great convention.

And I should like to say to my friends of the press and radio that I regret that I have no manuscript and have therefore been unable to give them an advance on what I shall say. What I shall say, therefore, shall be spoken from the heart and not from a piece of paper.

I have not had time, since I received this invitation, to write a speech and I know from my own experience—sometimes I make a better one when I have never written it out.

My friends, we who today represent the Democratic party in this convention are charged with a profound obligation. Millions of men and women are at this very hour watching the proceedings of this assembly. Four years ago there were approximately a million television sets in the United States with an average of about four people looking on in a million homes in the land.

Today there are seventeen million television sets in the United States with five or six looking on so that tonight and during this entire convention seventy million to ninety million people will be listening or looking at our deliberations here in this great convention.

And the television and the radio will have a more profound effect upon the verdict which the American people will render next November than at any other time in the history of this nation.

Four years ago, when I had the honor to be the temporary chairman of the Democratic convention in Philadelphia and to deliver the keynote address, I said to those assembled there that if we could get our message to the American people, if by every means at our hands we could give them the truth of our record and of our program, they would respond in 1948 as they had responded for sixteen years since 1932.

We were able to get our message to the people. We were able to bring to them the truth of our type of democracy, of our type of government, and they responded in 1948 as they had done since 1932 and I make the same prediction here tonight that if we can get our cause and the truth before the American people in 1952 they will again respond as they did in 1948.

Because they know and you know and I know that truth will make the people free.

They can be enslaved only by falsehoods and it is our duty as Democrats and as Americans charged with the responsibility of government, charged with the responsibility of bringing government to the people, it is our duty and our responsibility, by every means by which we may bring that truth to them, to bring it to them in all of its nakedness and all its sheer austerity so that they may know from us and not from our enemies alone the record of the Democratic party under the Roosevelt and Harry Truman administrations for the last twenty years.

My friends, democracy is not a mere political formula. Democracy and the yearning for democracy among the people not only of America but of the world is not bound by state borders or by national borders or international boundaries.

Democracy and freedom, as we understand them and want to enjoy them, are not circumscribed by religious denominations. They are not circumscribed by economic conditions. They are not circumscribed by race, creed or color—either here or elsewhere in the entire world.

While, of course, in part democracy and freedom represent a political formula, democracy and freedom are things of the spirit, as well as of the mind. They're things that appeal to the hopes and the ambitions and aspirations of mankind everywhere.

And I believe, as I believe that I'm standing here, and as I believe that this convention will give to the American people the next President and Vice President of the United States, I believe, I believe that without regard to forms of government, without regard to geography, without regard to religious, racial or original precedence or antecedents that 99 per cent of the world's population yearn for liberty, yearn for freedom, yearn that the shackles that now bind them may be loosed from their ankles and that they may stand forth erect before Almighty God and before mankind, free, independent men and women.

We also know that in the First Amendment to our Constitution as a part of the Bill of Rights we have separation of church and state organically in this nation.

We also know that democracy and religion are handmaids, they go together and there are innumerable instances in the life of every man and woman, and of every nation and every group, where it is not easy to determine the difference between a man's civic and his religious duty and we know also that in this great nation of ours, 175 years old, that our democracy, our freedom, our civilization, our way of life, have been founded upon and buttressed by the moral concept that is taught by religion among our people without regard to that religious denomination,

It is that sort of democratic conception for which the Democratic party, of which you and I are members, stand tonight. We have been taught to believe in and to observe freedom of worship, freedom of speech, freedom of the press, freedom of assembly. These are the fundamental four freedoms of our democracy, and of our civilization.

But, my friends, freedom of worship, freedom of speech, freedom of the press, freedom of assembly are but idle words unless we have freedom of thought—that men have the right to think and think out loud. Because out of the abundance of the heart, the mouth speaketh in democracy as well as everywhere in the world.

I'm here tonight, in what brief words I should utter, to try to present spiritual values of democracy. I'm here tonight in no narrow partisan spirit. I'm here tonight as an American first and a Democrat second.

I believe that the principles and policies in the program of the Democratic party—from Thomas Jefferson, its founder, to Harry Truman, its preserver—are the theories and the programs that bring the greatest good to the greatest number of the American people, and if I did not believe that I would join some other party I thought did believe in those eternal and immortal principles.

The Republican nominee for President of the United States in his acceptance speech delivered from this platform said that he was going to lead a great crusade, a new crusade by the Republican party, in connection with the Government of the United States.

Well, if he leads a crusade, or if the Republican party in this campaign indulges in a crusade, it will be new because they have never yet crusaded for anything that meant the welfare of the American people.

We are not beginning a crusade—we are continuing a crusade. We are continuing a crusade that we began twenty years ago and more, a crusade first to lift the American people out of the depths of a despair which had befallen them after twelve years of Republican inefficiency, ineptitude and mismanagement in the affairs of our nation; a crusade to set the farmer out of

the ditch of despondency, place his feet upon the firm foundation of economic equality with all other groups of our people;
a crusade to establish a sound and stable banking system; a crusade to give to the American people honest, free and efficient industry; a crusade to give to labor a new charter of liberty, so that
they might have the right with equal power and representation
to sit around the council table with their employers and adjust
their differences of wages and working conditions fairly and
honorably and honestly in the American spirit; a crusade to see
that every American had a decent home in which to live with not
only all of the necessaries of life, but some of the luxuries of life
as well; a crusade to see to it that every child born of woman
under the American flag should be born under conditions making it fairly easy for him to live in a normal, wholesome atmos-
phere with a chance for education to prepare himself for the
burdens and responsibilities of life; a crusade for all of our
people; a crusade to preserve the wasting soil of our land; a
crusade to protect our river valleys from destruction and waste
and damage; a crusade to give to every American farm home
the boon of electricity and lift the burden of housework in part
from the backs of the wives of farmers and give them the power
with which to produce the necessaries of life upon which we
subsist.

Not only a crusade to make our life happier and fuller and
freer, but a crusade likewise to bring peace and hope and cooperation among the nations and the peoples of the world so
that our inventive genius might not be turned toward the destruction of man and all of his works but toward the constructive activities that might mean a higher standard of life, a happier and fuller life for all mankind in the years that lie on
before.

Twenty years we have built or laid the foundations of an
edifice of equality and of justice to all classes of our people in
all parts of our country.

During that twenty years we have tried to build an edifice in
which all Americans might dwell with pride and satisfaction and
contentment in order that they might all not only have life, lib-

erty and the pursuit of happiness, but they might have life more abundantly, that they might have liberty and dignity and freedom, that they might not only pursue happiness, but overtake it and enjoy it and clutch it to their bosoms as free men have a right to do.

In the building of that edifice for labor, for agriculture, for honest business, for banking, in building that edifice of international trade and cooperation, so that the products of American labor might find markets among the working nations of the earth, in the construction of that edifice I am proud to have been a humble mechanic, laying here a brick and yonder a stone and yonder a joist, and here and there hanging the door in order that the people might come and go freely in that edifice built for them and for their advancement.

I do not know what the fate of the world holds for us. I have no crystal ball. I am no prophet. I cannot see into the future any more than any other man. But I know one thing, that in spite of its deficiencies, in spite of its acknowledged mistakes and defects, the administrations of Franklin D. Roosevelt and Harry S. Truman . . . [have] given the American people the greatest share in the enjoyment of the fruits of their labor than any other administration in the history of the United States.

I am proud to have been given the opportunity by the American people to play a humble part in that great work, and whether I ever hold another office, or whether I shall retire to the shades and shelters of private life, I shall carry to my dying day the cherished memory of that program, and so long as I shall breathe the breath of life I shall fight for these things in which I believe and you believe and in which the American people believe.

So much, my friends, for our domestic affairs. So much for the work we've tried to do for the American people. And let me dwell now for just a moment upon our international policies which affect the lives and the welfare of every home and every hearthstone and every family, and every man and woman and every boy and girl under the flag of the United States.

What may happen in the most remote and backward part of the world may affect our destiny and our welfare. The world today is divided three ways: one third of it living under democratic institutions; one third of it living under autocratic totalitarianism, and one third standing on tiptoe with shaded eye to scan the horizon to see what tomorrow may bring to them and to their children.

Twice in a generation we have been drawn unavoidably into great world wars. We have not sought other territory. We have not sought to take away from any people any economic or other life to which they have been entitled. We have sought peace. We have sought democracy. We have sought cooperation among the nations of the world.

At the end of World War I a great adventure was launched under the League of Nations but it became impotent and powerless to stop aggression and preserve the peace.

The League of Nations could not stop the Japanese when they invaded China. The League of Nations could not arrest Mussolini when he invaded Ethiopia. The League of Nations could not stop Hitler when he went into the Rhine and the Ruhr, into the Sudetenland, into Austria and finally crossed the Polish border and brought on World War II.

Into that war we were drawn to defend our institutions. Into that war we were drawn because there were no other honorable courses that we could pursue after the attack upon Pearl Harbor by the treacherous military clique of the Japanese Empire.

And when our Republicans say that under Democratic administrations there have been two great World Wars, I ask them to tell the American people what they would have done if they had been in power on December 7, 1941, when Pearl Harbor was attacked by the army of Japan.

At the end of World War II we undertook again to organize the world for peace through the United Nations. The United Nations is the second effort of mankind to organize the world for peace to preserve peace, to put down aggression.

And I say, as every man in this audience and America knows, that if the United Nations goes the way of the League of Nations the last hope of mankind to organize the world for peace will vanish in our day. And it may be for a century.

That's why we are in Korea. We are in Korea because we pledged our word in San Francisco that as a member of the United Nations we would come to the defense of any innocent nation unjustly attacked by an aggressor anywhere in the world.

Last November my wife and I journeyed to Korea. I had my Thanksgiving dinner with our men in uniform in Korea. Two days later I celebrated my birthday on the snow-clad mountains of Korea with the men in uniform. It was the last birthday I've ever had but it is not the last one I'll ever have by a number of years.

Before we got up on this mountain, which was beyond the Thirty-eighth Parallel, I said to General Ridgway, "I want to eat my birthday meal with the boys in the front." And when we arrived they had arranged a tent for me in which to eat my meal.

And I said I do not want to eat in this tent, I want to take my place in line with the rest of our soldiers and with my mess kit, take my share of food with them. I got my share of food. And on the snow-clad mountain we sat around in groups eating that food.

Over to my right was a Negro soldier from Birmingham, Alabama; to my left was a white soldier from Cincinnati, Ohio. In front of me was another Negro soldier from one of the Carolinas and behind me were white soldiers from all over the country.

And as we sat there and ate our food, I said to this Negro soldier from Birmingham, Alabama, "How do you like it over here?"

"Well," he said, "if I had my druthers, I'd ruther be back in Birmingham." "But," he said, "if they give me the green light I'm ready to march to that Yalu River no matter what the sacrifice may be."

And as I listened to that colored soldier in the uniform of the American Army telling me that he was ready, upon the flashing of the green light, to march to the Yalu River, I said I wish to Almighty God I could transmit some of the courage of his stout heart to some of the puny cowards in our own country, . . . [drowned out by applause] . . . political reasons which make it harder for him to march to the Yalu or to march to any other river which means the defense of our institutions, or civilization and the democracy of which we are proud.

My friends, let us not deceive ourselves. And let us not go astray by false gods and false doctrines and illusions. Let us not approach a mirage which has been the death of many a traveler in the deserts of the world.

The Republican party has put out a flashy and glamorous show-window in front of their place of business. Let us not be deceived by that flashy, glamorous show-window. Let the American people go inside and look on the shelves to see what sort of goods are on the shelves of the Republican show-house.

And when they do they will find that in spite of the flashy, glamorous show-window they will find on the shelves the same old shopworn, moth-eaten, tinsel, shoddy goods they have for the last generation peddled to the American people.

We will present these issues to the American people.

We will carry our message to Garcia and we'll find Garcia at home when we deliver that message on every doorstep, in every home in every section of America, and when they have heard that message and have learned that truth they will again respond not only in behalf of our great economic domestic problem but in behalf of our great foreign policy carried on in the first instance by Franklin D. Roosevelt and now by Harry S. Truman.

At home there has never been a more courageous President of the United States at any time in the history of America.

And when the American people shall have rendered their verdict in behalf of this great program, those people will go forward to complete this edifice of which I spoke a moment ago.

We shall have a fuller, happier, freer life in this nation and we shall present to the world peace and all mankind, all of the two and a half billion human beings who today are bowed down with the weight of taxation and the burden brought on by war and the fear of war until the day shall come when they shall all rise from their stooped posture, stand erect before Almighty God and before mankind as free men and women.

When that day comes we shall all rejoice without regard to position, without regard to politics, without regard to race, creed or color, without regard to economic conditions, we will all rejoice in our part in bringing these things to mankind, these things to the world.

God grant that it may come in your day and mine.

Thank you, and goodby.

ACCEPTANCE SPEECH [6]

ADLAI E. STEVENSON [7]

Governor Adlai E. Stevenson, of Illinois, gave this speech of acceptance, in nomination for the presidency, at the Democratic National Convention, Chicago, Illinois, at three o'clock on the morning of Saturday, July 26, 1952.

On the preceding Monday, Stevenson had given the welcoming speech to the convention and had undoubtedly stimulated the demand for his nomination.   Before the opening of the proceedings he had steadily denied his interest in the nomination. The turning point in the support for him came during the preceding Sunday when the Illinois delegation declared that it would vote for him. Pennsylvania echoed similar intent.

The leading candidates for the nomination were Estes Kefauver, with approximately 256 votes pledged to him; Richard B. Russell, with some 191; W. Averell Harriman, with some 10; and Stevenson with 41.

The preliminary issue before the convention was whether every state delegation would pledge support to whatever nominee was selected and would guarantee to have his name properly placed under the Democratic emblem for the November vote. A resolution for such pledge was debated. The Harriman group fought for the proposal; the Russellites strongly opposed; and the Stevenson forces, in the middle of the road, won out.

On the first ballot the groups held their lines firmly. On the second, Stevenson increased his following from 273 to 324, with the others holding their approximate strength. On the third, after New York and Massachusetts threw their votes to Stevenson, the band wagon developed and the Illinois governor was nominated. President Truman, who had arrived that day, introduced the new candidate.

Stevenson's speech was an extraordinary experience for those at the convention. The nominee's was a fresh, original voice, imaginative, witty. The speaker had a sense of the tragedy and direction of history. He was a figure of dignity. The speech was free from cliches and banalities. It was even more impressive than was Eisenhower's of two weeks previously.   Stevenson in the delivery was humble, calm, unpretentious, well keyed to visible audience, radio, and television.

The public were almost unanimous in proclaiming that the two conventions had achieved outstanding results in selecting as candidates two men of unusual integrity, stature, and ability before audiences.

[6] Text furnished through the courtesy of the Democratic National Committee.
[7] For biographical note, see Appendix.

Mr. President, Ladies and Gentlemen of the Convention, my Fellow Citizens:

I accept your nomination—and your program.

I should have preferred to hear those words uttered by a stronger, a wiser, a better man than myself. But after listening to the President's speech I even feel better about myself.

None of you, my friends, can wholly appreciate what is in my heart. I can only hope that you understand my words. They will be few.

I have not sought the honor you have done me. I could not seek it because I aspired to another office, which was the full measure of my ambition. And one does not treat the highest office within the gift of the people of Illinois as an alternative or as a consolation prize.

I would not seek your nomination for the presidency because the burdens of that office stagger the imagination. Its potential for good or evil now and in the years of our lives smothers exultation and converts vanity to prayer.

I have asked the Merciful Father, the Father of us all, to let this cup pass from me. But from such dread responsibility one does not shrink in fear, in self-interest, or in false humility.

So, "If this cup may not pass from me, except I drink it, Thy will be done."

That my heart has been troubled, that I have not sought this nomination, that I could not seek it in good conscience, that I would not seek it in honest self-appraisal, it is not to say that I value it the less. Rather it is that I revere the office of the presidency of the United States.

And now, my friends, that you have made your decision I will fight to win that office with all my heart and my soul. And with your help, I have no doubt that we will win.

You have summoned me to the highest mission within the gift of any people. I could not be more proud. Better men than I were at hand for this mighty task, and I owe to you and to them every resource of mind and of strength that I possess to make your deed today a good one for our country and for our party. I am confident, too, that your selection of a candidate for vice president will strengthen me and our party immeasurably in the hard, the implacable work that lies ahead of all of us.

I know you join me in gratitude and in respect for the great Democrats and the leaders of our generation whose names you have considered here in this convention, whose vigor, whose character and devotion to the Republic we love so well have won the respect of countless Americans and enriched our party.

I shall need them, we shall need them, because I have not changed in any respect since yesterday. Your nomination, awesome as I find it, has not enlarged my capacities. So I am profoundly grateful and emboldened by their comradeship and their fealty. And I have been deeply moved by their expressions of goodwill and of support. And I cannot, my friends, resist the urge to take the one opportunity that has been afforded me to pay my humble respects to a very great and good American whom I am proud to call my kinsman—Alben Barkley of Kentucky.

Let me say, too, that I have been heartened by the conduct of this convention. You have argued and disagreed because as Democrats you care and you care deeply. But you have disagreed and argued without calling each other liars and thieves, without despoiling our best traditions in any naked struggles for power.

And you have written a platform that neither equivocates, contradicts nor evades.

You have restated our party's record, its principles and its purposes in language that none can mistake, and with a firm confidence in justice, freedom and peace on earth that will raise the hearts and the hopes of mankind for that distant day when no one rattles a saber and no one drags a chain.

For all these things I am grateful to you. But I feel no exultation, no sense of triumph. Our troubles are all ahead of us.

Some will call us appeasers; others will say that we are the war party.

Some will say we are reactionary; others will say that we stand for socialism.

There will be the inevitable cries of "throw the rascals out"; "it's time for a change"; and so on and so on.

We'll hear all those things and many more besides. But we will hear nothing that we have not heard before. I am not too much concerned with partisan denunciation, with epithets and abuse, because the working man, the farmer, the thoughtful business man, all know that they are better off than ever before and they all know that the greatest danger to free enterprise in this country died with the great depression under the hammer blows of the Democratic party.

Nor am I afraid that the precious two-party system is in danger. Certainly the Republican party looked brutally alive a couple of weeks ago, and I mean both Republican parties!

Nor am I afraid that the Democratic party is old and fat and indolent. After 150 years it has been old for a long time; and it will never be indolent as long as it looks forward and not back, as long as it commands the allegiance of the young and the hopeful who dream the dreams and see the visions of a better America and a better world.

You will hear many sincere and thoughtful people express concern about the continuation of one party in power for twenty years. I don't belittle this attitude. But change for the sake of change has no absolute merit in itself.

If our greatest hazard is preservation of the values of Western civilization, in our self-interest alone, if you please, is it the part of wisdom to change for the sake of change to a party with a split personality; to a leader, whom we all respect, but who has been called upon to minister to a hopeless case of political schizophrenia?

If the fear is corruption in official position, do you believe with Charles Evans Hughes that guilt is personal and knows no party? Do you doubt the power of any political leader, if he has the will to do so, to set his own house in order without his neighbors having to burn it down?

What does concern me, in common with thinking partisans of both parties, is not just winning this election, but how it is won, how well we can take advantage of this great quadrennial opportunity to debate issues sensibly and soberly.

I hope and pray that we Democrats, win or lose, can campaign not as a crusade to exterminate the opposing party, as our opponents seem to prefer, but as a great opportunity to educate and elevate a people whose destiny is leadership, not alone of a rich and prosperous, contented country as in the past, but of a world in ferment.

And, my friends, more important than winning the election is governing the nation. That is the test of a political party— the acid, final test. When the tumult and the shouting die, when the bands are gone and the lights are dimmed, there is the stark reality of responsibility in an hour of history haunted with those gaunt, grim specters of strife, dissension and materialism at home, and ruthless, inscrutable and hostile power abroad.

The ordeal of the twentieth century—the bloodiest, most turbulent era of the Christian age—is far from over. Sacrifice, patience, understanding and implacable purpose may be our lot for years to come.

Let's face it. Let's talk sense to the American people. Let's tell them the truth, that there are no gains without pains, that we are now on the eve of great decisions, not easy decisions, like resistance when you're attacked, but a long, patient, costly struggle which alone can assure triumph over the great enemies of man— war, poverty and tyranny—and the assaults upon human dignity which are the most grievous consequences of each.

Let's tell them that the victory to be won in the twentieth century, this portal to the golden age, mocks the pretensions of individual acumen and ingenuity. For it is a citadel guarded by thick walls of ignorance and of mistrust which do not fall before the trumpets' blast or the politicians' imprecations or even a general's baton. They are, my friends, walls that must be directly stormed by the hosts of courage, of morality and of vision, standing shoulder to shoulder, unafraid of ugly truth, contemptuous of lies, half truths, circuses and demagoguery.

The people are wise—wiser than the Republicans think. And the Democratic party is the people's party, not the labor party, not the farmers' party, not the employers' party—it is the party of no one because it is the party of everyone.

That, I think, is our ancient mission. Where we have deserted it we have failed. With your help there will be no desertion now. Better we lose the election than mislead the people; and better we lose than misgovern the people.

Help me do the job in this autumn of conflict and of campaign; help me to do the job in these years of darkness, of doubt and of crisis which stretch beyond the horizon of tonight's happy vision, and we will justify our glorious past and the loyalty of silent millions who look to us for compassion, for understanding and for honest purpose. Thus we will serve our great tradition greatly.

I ask of you all you have; I will give to you all I have, even as he who came here tonight and honored me, as he has honored you—the Democratic party—by a lifetime of service and bravery that will find him an imperishable page in the history of the Republic and of the Democratic party—President Harry S. Truman.

And finally, my friends, in the staggering task that you have assigned me, I shall always try "to do justly, to love mercy and to walk humbly with my God."

APOLOGIA [8]

RICHARD M. NIXON [9]

Senator Richard M. Nixon broadcast this address from Los Angeles by radio and TV on September 23, 1952. It was a defense of his use of some $18,000, received from a group of supporters during the previous two years. Who gave the money? The issue was, Was the fund used for personal rather than senatorial expenses? And did the fund influence the Senator in his decisions concerning public questions?

On September 18, the New York *Post* revealed the main facts concerning the fund. Immediately the Republican leaders, with their playing up of corruption as a main campaign issue, raised the question of whether Nixon should resign. Eisenhower announced that he would await Nixon's explanation.

The speech was one of self-vindication, filled with ethical proof, with every attribute of persuasiveness. There was concrete explanation of his use of the fund; highly personal treatment throughout as he recited his earlier career and the part played in it by "Pat"; deep seriousness, frankness, sense of moral indignation; clever transition from a purely defensive position to that of strong denunciation of the Democratic policies; effective oral style (note the repetition and loose constructions); and highly effective extempore delivery. The earlier experience of Nixon as college debater, his former political campaigning, his speaking career in the House and Senate and as member of the House Un-American Affairs Committee—all were told off to his advantage in this crucial test of September 23. With the aid of a few notes he pleaded his case, at first sitting composedly, later rising and gesticulating toward his screen audience.

The speech aimed at action. The speaker cleverly made the general public his jury—("Wire and write the Republican National Committee, . . . Whatever their decision is, I will abide by it.")

Hostile critics regarded the speech as so much "soap opera," presented with dramatic tones, a speech filled with details calculated to move each listener ("Pat is not a quitter. After all, her name was Patricia Ryan and she was born on St. Patrick's Day, and you know the Irish never quit.")

Among the millions who listened and observed were fifteen thousand in Cleveland's Civic Auditorium. Many there wept as Nixon concluded. Eisenhower, before the audience, said, "I saw an example of courage." Telegrams at the rate of four thousand per hour poured in to the Na-

[8] From a recording by the editor.

[9] For biographical note, see Appendix.

tional Republican Headquarters in Washington—more than 150,000 in two days. Obviously, Nixon could sway audiences. Soap opera or not, it was a remarkable triumph for the young California candidate.

At Wheeling, West Virginia, on Wednesday night, September 24, the two candidates met. Eisenhower told the rally that Nixon had been "completely vindicated."

The entire incident no doubt furthered the Republican cause in the campaign of 1952.

My fellow Americans: I come before you tonight as a candidate for the vice presidency and as a man whose honesty and integrity has been questioned.

Now, the usual political thing to do when charges are made against you is to either ignore them or to deny them without giving details. I believe we have had enough of that in the United States, particularly with the present Administration in Washington, D.C.

To me the office of the vice presidency of the United States is a great office, and I feel that the people have got to have confidence in the integrity of the men who run for that office and who might attain them.

I have a theory, too, that the best and only answer to a smear or to an honest misunderstanding of the facts is to tell the truth. And that is why I am here tonight. I want to tell you my side of the case.

I am sure that you have read the charge, and you have heard it, that I, Senator Nixon, took $18,000 from a group of my supporters.

Now, was that wrong? And let me say that it was wrong— I am saying it, incidentally, that it was wrong, not just illegal, because it isn't a question of whether it was legal or illegal, that isn't enough. The question is, Was it morally wrong? I say that it was morally wrong—if any of that $18,000 went to Senator Nixon, for my personal use. I say that it was morally wrong if it was secretly given and secretly handled. And I say that it was morally wrong if any of the contributors got special favors for the contributions that they made.

And now to answer those questions let me say this:

Not one cent of the $18,000 or any other money of that type ever went to me for my personal use. Every penny of it was used to pay for political expenses that I did not think should be charged to the taxpayers of the United States.

It was not a secret fund. As a matter of fact, when I was on "Meet the Press," some of you may have seen it last Sunday —Peter Edson came up to me after the program and he said, "Dick, what about this fund we hear about?" And I said, Well, there's no secret about it. Go out and see Dana Smith, who was the administrator of the fund. And I gave him his address, and I said that you will find that the purpose of the fund simply was to defray political expenses that I did not feel should be charged to the Government.

And third, let me point out, and I want to make this particularly clear, that no contributor to this fund, no contributor to any of my campaign, has ever received any consideration that he would not have received as an ordinary constituent.

I just don't believe in that and I can say that never, while I have been in the Senate of the United States, as far as the people that contributed to this fund are concerned, have I made a telephone call for them to an agency, or have I gone down to an agency in their behalf. And the record will show that, the records which are in the hands of the Administration.

But then some of you will say and rightly, "Well, what did you use the fund for, Senator? Why did you have to have it?"

Let me tell you in just a word how a Senate office operates. First of all, a senator gets $15,000 a year in salary. He gets enough money to pay for one trip a year, a round trip that is, for himself and his family between his home and Washington, D.C.

And then he gets an allowance to handle the people that work in his office, to handle his mail. And the allowance for my state of California is enough to hire thirteen people.

And let me say, incidentally, that that allowance is not paid to the senator—it's paid directly to the individuals that the senator puts on his payroll, that all of these people and all of these allowances are for strictly official business. Business, for example, when a constituent writes in and wants you to go down to the Veterans Administration and get some information about his GI policy. Items of that type for example.

But there are other expenses which are not covered by the Government. And I think I can best discuss those expenses by asking you some questions. Do you think that when I or any other senator makes a political speech, has it printed, should charge the printing of that speech and the mailing of that speech to the taxpayers?

Do you think, for example, when I or any other senator makes a trip to his home state to make a purely political speech that the cost of that trip should be charged to the taxpayers?

Do you think when a senator makes political broadcasts or political television broadcasts, radio or television, that the expense of those broadcasts should be charged to the taxpayer?

Well, I know what your answer is. The same answer that audiences give me whenever I discuss this particular problem. The answer is, No. The taxpayers shouldn't be required to finance items which are not official business but which are primarily political business.

But then the question arises, you say, "Well, how do you pay for these and how can you do it legally?"

And there are several ways that it can be done, incidentally, and that it is done legally in the United States Senate and in the Congress.

The first way is to be a rich man. I don't happen to be a rich man so I couldn't use that.

Another way that is used is to put your wife on the payroll. Let me say, incidentally, my opponent, my opposite number for the vice presidency on the Democratic ticket, does have his wife on the payroll. And has had her on his payroll for the ten years —the past ten years.

Now just let me say this. That's his business and I'm not critical of him for doing that. You will have to pass judgment on that particular point. But I have never done that for this reason. I have found that there are so many deserving stenographers and secretaries in Washington that needed the work that I just didn't feel it was right to put my wife on the payroll.

My wife's sitting over here. She's a wonderful stenographer. She used to teach stenography and she used to teach shorthand in high school. That was when I met her. And I can tell you folks that she's worked many hours at night and many hours on Saturdays and Sundays in my office and she's done a fine job. And I'm proud to say tonight that in the six years I've been in the House and the Senate of the United States, Pat Nixon has never been on the Government payroll.

There are other ways that these finances can be taken care of. Some who are lawyers, and I happen to be a lawyer, continue to practice law. But I haven't been able to do that. I'm so far away from California that I've been so busy with my senatorial work that I have not engaged in any legal practice.

And also as far as law practice is concerned, it seemed to me that the relationship between an attorney and the client was so personal that you couldn't possibly represent a man as an attorney and then have an unbiased view when he presented his case to you in the event that he had one before the Government.

And so I felt that the best way to handle these necessary political expenses of getting my message to the American people and the speeches I made, the speeches that I had printed, for the most part, concerned this one message—of exposing this Administration, the communism in it, the corruption in it—the only way that I could do that was to accept the aid which people in my home state of California who contributed to my campaign and who continued to make these contributions after I was elected were glad to make.

And let me say I am proud of the fact that not one of them has ever asked me for a special favor. I'm proud of the fact that not one of them has ever asked me to vote on a bill other than as my own conscience would dictate. And I am proud of the fact that the taxpayers by subterfuge or otherwise have never paid one dime for expenses which I thought were political and shouldn't be charged to the taxpayers.

Let me say, incidentally, that some of you may say, "Well, that's all right, Senator; that's your explanation, but have you got any proof?"

And I'd like to tell you this evening that just about an hour ago we received an independent audit of this entire fund.

I suggested to Governor Sherman Adams, who is the chief of staff of the Dwight Eisenhower campaign, that an independent audit and legal report be obtained. And I have that audit here in my hand.

It's an audit made by the Price, Waterhouse & Co. firm, and the legal opinion by Gibson, Dunn & Crutcher, lawyers in Los Angeles, the biggest law firm and incidentally one of the best ones in Los Angeles.

I'm proud to be able to report to you tonight that this audit and this legal opinion is being forwarded to General Eisenhower. And I'd like to read to you the opinion that was prepared by Gibson, Dunn & Crutcher and based on all the pertinent laws and statutes, together with the audit report prepared by the certified public accountants.

It is our conclusion that Senator Nixon did not obtain any financial gain from the collection and disbursement of the fund by Dana Smith; that Senator Nixon did not violate any Federal or state law by reason of the operation of the fund, and that neither the portion of the fund paid by Dana Smith directly to third persons nor the portion paid to Senator Nixon to reimburse him for designated office expenses constituted income to the Senator which was either reportable or taxable as income under applicable tax laws. (Signed) Gibson, Dunn & Crutcher by Alma H. Conway.

Now that, my friends, is not Nixon speaking, but that's an independent audit which was requested because I want the American people to know all the facts and I'm not afraid of having independent people go in and check the facts, and that is exactly what they did.

But then I realize that there are still some who may say, and rightly so, and let me say that I recognize that some will continue to smear regardless of what the truth may be, but that there has been understandably some honest misunderstanding on this matter, and there's some that will say:

"Well, maybe you were able, Senator, to fake this thing. How can we believe what you say? After all, is there a possibility that you may have feathered your own nest?"

And so now what I am going to do—and incidentally this is unprecedented in the history of American politics—I am going at this time to give to this television and radio audience a complete financial history; everything I've earned; everything I've spent; everything I owe. And I want you to know the facts. I'll have to start early.

I was born in 1913. Our family was one of modest circumstances and most of my early life was spent in a store out in East Whittier. It was a grocery store—one of those family enterprises. The only reason we were able to make it go was because my mother and dad had five boys and we all worked in the store.

I worked my way through college and to a great extent through law school. And then, in 1940, probably the best thing that ever happened to me happened, I married Pat—sitting over here. We had a rather difficult time after we were married, like so many of the young couples who may be listening to us. I practiced law; she continued to teach school. I went into the service.

Let me say that my service record was not a particularly unusual one. I went to the South Pacific. I guess I'm entitled to a couple of battle stars. I got a couple of letters of commendation but I was just there when the bombs were falling and then I returned. I returned to the United States and in 1946 I ran for the Congress.

When we came out of the war, Pat and I—Pat during the war had worked as a stenographer and in a bank and as an economist for a Governmental agency—and when we came out the total of our savings from both my law practice, her teaching and all the time that I was in the war—the total for that entire period was just a little less than $10,000. Every cent of that, incidentally, was in Government bonds.

Well, that's where we start when I go into politics. Now what have I earned since I went into politics? Well, here it is— I jotted it down, let me read the notes. First of all I've had my salary as a congressman and as a senator. Second, I have received a total in this past six years of $1,600 from estates which were in my law firm at the time that I severed my connection with it.

And, incidentally, as I said before, I have not engaged in any legal practice and have not accepted any fees from business that came into the firm after I went into politics. I have made an average of approximately $1,500 a year from nonpolitical speaking engagements and lectures. And then, fortunately, we've inherited a little money. Pat sold her interest in her father's estate for $3,000 and I inherited $1,500 from my grandfather.

We live rather modestly. For four years we lived in an apartment in Park Fairfax, in Alexandria, Va. The rent was $80 a month. And we saved for the time that we could buy a house.

Now, that was what we took in. What did we do with this money? What do we have today to show for it? This will surprise you, because it is so little, I suppose, as standards generally go, of people in public life. First of all, we've got a house in Washington which cost $41,000 and on which we owe $20,000.

We have a house in Whittier, California, which cost $13,000 and on which we owe $10,000. My folks are living there at the present time.

I have just $4,000 in life insurance, plus my GI policy which I've never been able to convert and which will run out in two years. I have no life insurance whatever on Pat. I have no life insurance on our two youngsters, Patricia and Julie. I own a 1950 Oldsmobile car. We have our furniture. We have no stocks and bonds of any type. We have no interest of any kind, direct or indirect, in any business.

Now, that's what we have. What do we owe? Well, in addition to the mortgage, the $20,000 mortgage on the house in Washington, the $10,000 one on the house in Whittier, I owe $4,500 to the Riggs Bank in Washington, D.C. with interest 4½ per cent.

I owe $3,500 to my parents and the interest on that loan which I pay regularly, because it's the part of the savings they made through the years they were working so hard, I pay regularly 4 per cent interest. And then I have a $500 loan which I have on my life insurance.

Well, that's about it. That's what we have and that's what we owe. It isn't very much but Pat and I have the satisfaction that every dime that we've got is honestly ours. I should say this—that Pat doesn't have a mink coat. But she does have a respectable Republican cloth coat. And I always tell her that she'd look good in anything.

One other thing I probably should tell you because if I don't they'll probably be saying this about me too, we did get something—a gift—after the election. A man down in Texas heard Pat on the radio mention the fact that our two youngsters would like to have a dog. And, believe it or not, the day before we left on this campaign trip we got a message from Union Station in Baltimore saying they had a package for us. We went down to get it. You know what it was?

It was a little cocker spaniel dog, in a crate that he had sent all the way from Texas, black and white, spotted, and our little girl, Tricia, the six-year-old, named it Checkers.

And, you know, the kids, like all kids, loved the dog, and I just want to say this, right now, that regardless of what they say about it, we are going to keep it.

It isn't easy to come before a nation-wide audience and bare your life, as I have done. But I want to say some things before I conclude, that I think most of you will agree on.

Mr. Mitchell, the Chairman of the Democratic National Committee, made the statement that if a man couldn't afford to be in the United States Senate, he shouldn't run for the Senate. And I just want to make my position clear.

I don't agree with Mr. Mitchell when he says that only a rich man should serve his Government, in the United States Senate or in the Congress. I don't believe that represents the thinking of the Democratic party, and I know it doesn't represent the thinking of the Republican party.

I believe that it's fine that a man like Governor Stevenson, who inherited a fortune from his father, can run for President. But I also feel that it is essential in this country of ours that a man of modest means can also run for President, because, you know—remember Abraham Lincoln—you remember what he said—"God must have loved the common people, he made so many of them."

And now I'm going to suggest some courses of conduct.

First of all, you have read in the papers about other funds, now. Mr. Stevenson apparently had a couple. One of them in which a group of business people paid and helped to supplement the salaries of state employees. Here is where the money went directly into their pockets, and I think that what Mr. Stevenson should do should be to come before the American people, as I have, give the names of the people that contributed to that fund, give the names of the people who put this money into their pockets, at the same time that they were receiving money from their state government and see what favors, if any, they gave out for that.

I don't condemn Mr. Stevenson for what he did, but until the facts are in there is a doubt that would be raised. And as far as Mr. Sparkman is concerned, I would suggest the same thing. He's had his wife on the payroll. I don't condemn him for that, but I think that he should come before the American people and indicate what outside sources of income he has had. I would suggest that under the circumstances both Mr. Sparkman and Mr. Stevenson should come before the American people, as I have, and make a complete financial statement as to their financial history, and if they don't it will be an admission that they have something to hide.

And I think you will agree with me—because, folks, remember, a man that's to be President of the United States, a man that is to be Vice President of the United States, must have the confidence of all the people. And that's why I'm doing what I'm doing, and that is why I suggest that Mr. Stevenson and Mr. Sparkman, if they are under attack, that should be what they are doing.

Now, let me say this: I know that this is not the last of the smears. In spite of my explanation tonight, other smears will be made. Others have been made in the past. And the purpose of the smears, I know, is this, to silence me, to make me let up.

Well, they just don't know who they are dealing with. I'm going to tell you this: I remember, in the dark days of the Hiss trial, some of the same columnists, some of the same radio commentators who are attacking me now and misrepresenting my position, were violently opposing me at the time I was after Alger Hiss. But I continued to fight, because I knew I was right, and I can say to this great television and radio audience that I have no apologies to the American people for my part in putting

Alger Hiss where he is today. And as far as this is concerned, I intend to continue to fight.

Why do I feel so deeply? Why do I feel that in spite of the smears, the misunderstanding, the necessity for a man to come up here and bare his soul, as I have—why is it necessary for me to continue this fight? And I want to tell you why.

Because, you see, I love my country. And I think my country is in danger. And I think the only man that can save America at this time is the man that's running for President, on my ticket, Dwight Eisenhower. . . .

AMERICA'S ROLE [10]

ADLAI E. STEVENSON [11]

Governor Adlai E. Stevenson gave this address before an overflow crowd in the Mormon Tabernacle, Salt Lake City, on the evening of October 14, 1952. The address was delivered over radio and television. The audience broke into applause at almost every sentence.

The address was formal—more thoughtful, philosophical, than most of his other speeches. It was leagues removed from the informal whistle-stop utterances and was pretty much devoid of the witticisms and levity of many of his speeches. This address, by contrast, had the solemnity suggested by the surroundings, maturity of thinking and appeal hardly consonant with rough-and-tumble campaign debating. It was superior in conception and composition but hardly designed to move the average, more unsophisticated listeners.

The issue in this case was that of procedure in our foreign policy with respect to Korea and Europe and in our domestic policy with respect to social security and similar programs. In other speeches Stevenson became concrete, concerning corruption, labor, Korea, inflation, and other problems. Here he relied on the intelligence of his group to appraise properly his statement of our fundamental political principles.

This speech, like most of his others, was free from slogans or rallying cries. It was free from bombast, or from his usual lightness. Its language was formal, eloquent, original. Apparently he worried little about "talking over the heads of his listeners."

In this address is comparatively little or none of extended example, dialogue, narrative, or similar devices to enhance the comprehension, interest, and appeal.

The delivery, here, was accompanied by little bodily gesture. It was conversational, without shouting or demonstrativeness.

These tendencies would explain why Stevenson was far more effective over the radio than in face-to-face situations.

Whereas Eisenhower was superior in whistle-stopping where his vigor and resourcefulness could have full play, Stevenson resorted to television as the easiest way to make his name and person well known over the land. (His trial run in whistle-stopping convinced him that television and radio were necessary if he was to match Eisenhower in popularity in the months remaining.) A gifted extempore speaker, Stevenson could approach issues simply and clearly over the broad-casting systems. His personality was also agreeable to TV observers.

[10] Text furnished through the courtesy of the Democratic National Committee.
[11] For biographical note, see Appendix.

Polls indicated that his half-hour talks were highly favorably received. Hence he concentrated on that art medium. He accomplished results as favorable to his cause as might have been anticipated.

I cannot speak tonight in this tabernacle without an awareness of the links between its history and that of the State from which I come.

Many of us who reside in Illinois have tasted the wholesome tonic of humility in contemplation of the mistakes to which our history bears witness at Nauvoo—the beautiful place—on the Mississippi River where your forefathers stopped on their long journey and built another temple.

It was 106 years ago now that there were those "burnings," the persecution, the mob violence and the murders which finally drove the men and women of the Mormon faith on westward.

Now today this tabernacle, rising above this city and these fertile lands where men said nothing could ever grow, stands as a living monument to the inevitable triumph of faith. And when the caravans of those who today seek public office in this nation stop here with you, to meet with you in this, your tabernacle, they stop their clamor and haranguing. They seek the response of your hearts and your minds rather than that of your hands or your voices.

I wish that all of our political campaigning could be conducted in the spirit which this meeting place inspires. It is a spirit of faith, a faith that triumphs over any obstacle.

And tonight I want to talk in this temple to the great confident majority of Americans—the generous and the unfrightened, those who are proud of our strength and sure of our goodness and who want to work with each other in trust, to advance the honor of our country.

Needless to say this includes many millions of Republicans. If all virtue were in one party the nation would be in a sad way. But this confident majority, I am sorry to say, does not include the Republican speechmakers of this campaign. How do they picture our magnificent America?

Sometimes they whine about our troubles—describing us as choosing to live alone, friendless, on a remote island, indifferent to the fate of man, a huge hermit crab lacking a soul.

Sometimes they call large sections of us dupes and fellow-travelers—a people without a purpose and without a mind.

But at all times they picture us unworthily. They make us look scared, stupid, and heartless. They thus betray the conquering, hopeful, practical yet deeply moral America which you and I know.

There was a day when my opponent for the office of the presidency of these United States symbolized this grand nation of vast horizons and dazzling success. But now, for the sake of power, what has he not permitted himself? Far worse than his surrender to Taft, far worse than his acceptance of all the bad senators of his party, is what he said about American prosperity. He dared to tell us that our surge forward since 1945 has been based on war and on rearmament. And he implied that the whole growth of social justice during the past twenty years is also based on war.

This is the most unkind untruth of all, for this is the Kremlin story, this is the theme song of every Communist paper in France and Italy, and across the Iron Curtain. The prediction that this must be true, that our so-called "corrupt American capitalism" cannot survive, cannot prevent mass unemployment without war or the threat of war—this is written into every Marxian textbook. But why should the General suddenly accept it?

We all know it is nonsense, that in fact the reverse is true. To the dismay of the enemies of America, we proved after 1945 that we have learned in the last twenty years not only to produce majestically, but to distribute among all our people an increasingly fair share of that production. We have evolved a stronger and a better form of economy, which makes nonsense of the Russian textbooks.

The friends of freedom everywhere have rejoiced. They have noted our rising and widespread wealth and well-being. They have noted that we had no depression and no unemployment at the end of the war—in spite of headlong demobilization and disarmament. And remember that all this happened before the Marshall Plan, before the revival of our armed might, before Korea. Every liberty-loving European gave thanks that we had showed ourselves not only strong but stable.

Must this inspiring record now be ridiculed for campaign purposes? Must our credit for using our capitalist system wisely and humanely be undermined in Europe—and by General Eisenhower of all men? Must our proud all-American achievement be pictured as a Democratic party plot?

This must be somewhere near the low-water mark in the great American business of vote-getting, which has too often yielded more noise than light.

My friends, we dare not underplay our national greatness for these mean motives. During the war, you remember, when we all knew America was in danger, we only wanted the best, the most unselfish. We had no time for building political mantraps or for inventing derogatory tales. It was a heart-lifting moment, a noble experience to be one of the American people, at the top of our power, bound together in determination and mutual respect. There was a moral excitement to life in those days, in spite of the bitter loss and pain of war, which we shall never forget.

But a "cold war" leads the timid and the discontented into frustration. And out of frustration comes pettiness—the niggling pitiful picture of a confused, divided country which these Republican speechmakers are now painting. And this, of course, was the very purpose for which the Russians invented "cold war" and imposed it upon us.

They hoped we would feel frustrated, shackled by circumstance. They hoped we would fall to quarreling among ourselves and thus betray our mission.

But the American giant will not be shackled. We have only to examine these temptations, to which the "cold war" exposes us, to feel refreshed in our faith—and to feel sorry for the few among us who do not rise to this exacting test.

The first temptation is to be half regretful, half ashamed of our strength—or frightened of it, which is worse. Regretful

(God help us) in the face of the stirring truth that Lincoln's vision has come true, that now we are indeed the "last, best hope of earth"—so recognized by all the free world, which implores us to be great, to lead with magnanimity, and above all with patience. The very powerful, if they are good, must always be patient.

And still some of us regret it. Some of us say: "Why can't life leave us alone? We don't want to lead. We want to be undisturbed."

What would our fathers have said of such talk? From the dawn of our revolution they saw America as the old world's saviour—not merely in terms of power, but in terms of goodness.

They knew that Providence had given us this empty, unexploited continent for a purpose. And they knew that it must be a purpose which includes all men—for the same God made us all.

In 1787 George Washington said: "The preservation of the sacred fire of liberty, and the destiny of the republican form of government, are justly considered as deeply, perhaps as finally staked, on the experiment entrusted to the hands of the American people."

At that time we had less four million inhabitants. But there was no doubt, no fear, in Washington's mind regarding our destiny.

In 1858 Abraham Lincoln said: "Our reliance is in the love of liberty which God has planted in us. Our defense is in the spirit which prized liberty as the heritage of all men, in all lands everywhere."

At that time there were about thirty million Americans. And we were threatened with civil war. But there was no doubt, no fear, in Lincoln's mind. He saw the war and the dissolution of the union as a threat to the new, revolutionary idea of the free men and to democratic aspirations everywhere.

In 1915 Woodrow Wilson said: "The interesting and inspiring thought about America is that she asks nothing for herself except what she has a right to ask for humanity itself."

By that time we were a world power, about to enter into a world war. But there was no doubt, no fear, in Woodrow Wilson's mind. He knew, as in truth we have always known, that we were destined to be an example and to assume the burden of greatness.

So we are marked men, we Americans at the midcentury point. We have been tapped by fate—for which we should forever give thanks, not laments. What a day to live in. What a flowering of the work and the faith of our fathers. Who in heaven's name would want America less strong, less responsible for the future? Isn't this what we have always dreamed? To whom else would we choose to hand the torch of the free world?

And precisely because we are tapped by fate, we must be wise and patient as well as rich and strong. This means that we must live, intensely live, the faith which has made us free and thereby invincible. "Despotism may govern without faith, but liberty cannot."

American power is not just coal and iron and oil, cotton and wheat and corn. It is not just our forests and our mountain ranges, and the huge meandering rivers of our central plains, and the high, dry cattle country, and this lucky land of yours between the mountains and the ocean. It is not even all these things plus 160 million people. It is these things plus the people, plus the idea. For again, "despotism may govern without a faith, but liberty cannot."

So the second temptation of the cold, frustrating war—which we also proudly reject—is to become so distracted by our trouble that we take this faith too much for granted, that we salute it (as some of us salute our religion), and then go our way unchanged. If we do not make it part of us—keep it forever before us, intense and demanding and clear—the faith might die and we should then die with it.

What is this "American idea" which we so justly venerate? I suggest that the heart of it is the simple but challenging statement that no government may interfere with our conscience, may tell us what to think. All our freedoms, all our dynamic unleashed energies, stem from this.

We just naturally talk like this: "No government can tell me what to think. No government can tell me what to do, unless it can prove that the common good is served by such interference." This is the American way of living.

But government, keeping its hand most carefully away from that forbidden field, may and indeed must play its part in our steady national effort to promote welfare and to diminish hardship. Our government, we Democrats have always insisted, is a friendly, helpful force, to serve and to keep order, never to dominate, never to usurp our private lives.

Yet the same Republicans (the dinosaur-wing of that party) who object to service from our government—who call everything "creeping socialism," who talk darkly of "dictatorship"—these same men begin to hint that we are "subversive," or at best the tools of our country's enemies, when we boast of the great strides toward social justice and security we have already made, and of the still greater strides we plan. They laugh at us, superciliously, when we say we are the political party with a heart.

To honor and uphold our faith, therefore, we must never let them confuse us about the difference between what government should do if possible, and what it must never do if America is to survive.

It should strengthen us in our freedom by fostering as much widespread ownership and economic independence as possible. In the towns and counties, in the state capitals and in Washington, that great work goes forward today.

But never must government step across the line which separates the promotion of justice and prosperity from the interference with thought, with conscience, with the sacred private life of the mind.

If you like, this is the distinction between the things that are God's and the things that are Caesar's. The mind is the expression of the soul, which belongs to God and must be let alone by government. But farm prices, minimum wages, old-age pensions, the regulation of monopoly, the physical safety of society—these things are Caesar's province, wherein the government should do all that is humanly possible.

But those among us who would bar us from attempting our economic and social duty are quick with accusations, with defamatory hints and whispering campaigns, when they see a chance to scare or silence those with whom they disagree. Rudely, carelessly they invade the field of conscience, of thought—the field which belongs to God and not to senators—and not to protect the republic, but to discredit the individual.

Let us remember also that the first of the seven deadly sins is spiritual pride: the sin which assures me that I know and you don't, so that I give myself permission to use any dubious or dishonest means to discredit your opinion. Because we have always thought of government as friendly, not as brutal, character assassins and slanderers in the Congress of the United States have a free hand in the methods they use. We never foresaw that the cult of thought-control and of the big lie would come to America. So if their conscience permits, they can say almost anything. And if my opponent's conscience permits, he can try to help all of them get reelected. But will he have strengthened or weakened the American idea?

For this is no small thing, this remorseless attack upon freedom of conscience, freedom of thought. A few peddlers of hate and fear would be of little consequence if they had not been welcomed as satellites by Senator Taft and included in the leadership of this strange crusade. And none of them would be significant if the General—who was implored to come home by Republican leaders so that they might be quit of Senator Taft—had not yielded to the demands of his beaten foe. But because of that surrender, because of those strange allies in his queer crusade, our role in world history, our faithfulness to the men who made the United States, is challenged in this election.

Finally, then, let us recall that our basic faith in liberty of conscience has an ancient ancestry. We can trace it back through Christian Europe, and through pagan Rome, back to the Old Testament prophets. It is by no means exclusive with us. It is in fact our bond of unity with all free men. But we are its ordained guardians today.

Let us lift up our hearts, therefore—glad of our strength, proud of the task it imposes. So far from being half-defeated, half-divided, half-bankrupt—while we are true to ourselves we can never be defeated; while we accept the honorable burden of leadership, we can never be divided. And in the name of that burden we shall find the means and the determination to spend in money and in labor and in hard thought whatever is needed to save ourselves and our world.

CRUSADE FOR PEACE [12]

DWIGHT D. EISENHOWER [13]

General Dwight D. Eisenhower gave this speech at a Republican rally at the Masonic Auditorium in Detroit, on the evening of October 24, 1952. It was broadcast and telecast over the facilities of the National Broadcasting (Television) and the Columbia Broadcasting (Radio) systems.

The issue of the speech was, "What foreign policy shall we follow to end the Korean war?"

The question had been initiated by Eisenhower in his talk at the American Legion Convention in New York City, on August 25, and had been expanded in his Philadelphia address on September 4. More and more the problem loomed up as a crucial campaign issue. National sentiment demanded some answer to the problem of the sacrifices in Korea.

The Detroit speech had the merit of concreteness and inclusion of damning evidence. The responsibility of the Democratic administration for creating conditions that invited the Communist attack of June 1950 was presented with great conviction and persuasion. Stevenson and other Democrats immediately replied to this Eisenhower argument. The subsequent development of this phase of the debate up to the eve of the election was held to be in favor of the Republicans. Most voters, according to the polls, endorsed the analysis and solution as delineated in the Detroit address rather than those of the defenders of the Truman-Acheson Far East policies.

Although this Detroit speech bore many marks of ghost writing, the General's individual stamp was obvious. Military strategy and policy were themes on which he could talk endlessly and with deep conviction. (No doubt the personal proof evident throughout this speech carried great weight with the millions of Americans.) The General was at his best in whistle stop or other occasions when he was free from manuscripts (as when he addressed the Cleveland audience after listening to and seeing Nixon's "apologia").

Eisenhower was—and is—a highly effective extempore speaker. He obviously lacked Stevenson's originality and smoothness of phrase that would make good reading, but, the General, on the other hand, reacted with unusual physical and emotional vigor to his convictions. Thus delivered with considerable intensity and with a personality aglow with

---

[12] Text was supplied through the courtesy of the Republican National Committee and was checked with the tape recording.

[13] For biographical note, see Appendix.

his stand, his campaign speeches often evoked strong audience response. His voice and articulation were those of the Middle West. His gestures were briefly those of a pounding fist. He spoke as a soldier—direct, unaffected, and free from all elocutionary arts.

In this anxious autumn for America, one fact looms above all others in our people's mind. One tragedy challenges all men dedicated to the work of peace. One word shouts denial to those who foolishly pretend that ours is not a nation at war.

This fact, this tragedy, this word is: Korea.

A small country, Korea has been, for more than two years, the battleground for the costliest foreign war our nation has fought, excepting the two world wars. It has been the burial ground for twenty thousand American dead. It has been another historic field of honor for the valor and skill and tenacity of American soldiers.

All these things it has been—and yet one thing more. It has been a symbol—a telling symbol—of the foreign policy of our nation.

It has been a sign—a warning sign—of the way the Administration has conducted our world affairs.

It has been a measure—a damning measure—of the quality of leadership we have been given.

Tonight I am going to talk about our foreign policy and of its supreme symbol—the Korean war. I am not going to give you elaborate generalizations—but hard, tough facts. I am going to state the unvarnished truth.

What, then, are the plain facts?

The biggest fact about the Korean war is this: It was never inevitable, it was never inescapable, no fantastic fiat of history decreed that little South Korea—in the summer of 1950—would fatally tempt Communist aggressors as their easiest victim. No demonic destiny decreed that America had to be bled this way in order to keep South Korea free and to keep freedom itself self-respecting.

We are not mute prisoners of history. That is a doctrine for totalitarians, it is no creed for free men.

There is a Korean war—and we are fighting it—for the simplest of reasons: Because free leadership failed to check and to turn back Communist ambition before it savagely attacked us. The Korean war—more perhaps than any other war in history—simply and swiftly followed the collapse of our political defenses. There is no other reason than this: We failed to read and to outwit the totalitarian mind.

I know something of this totalitarian mind. Through the years of World War II, I carried a heavy burden of decision in the free world's crusade against the tyranny then threatening us all. Month after month, year after year, I had to search out and to weigh the strengths and weaknesses of an enemy driven by the lust to rule the great globe itself.

World War II should have taught us all one lesson. The lesson is this: To vacillate, to hesitate—to appease even by merely betraying unsteady purpose—is to feed a dictator's appetite for conquest and to invite war itself.

That lesson—which should have firmly guided every great decision of our leadership through these later years—was ignored in the development of the Administration's policies for Asia since the end of World War II. Because it was ignored, the record of these policies is a record of appalling failure.

The record of failure dates back—with red-letter folly—at least to September of 1947. It was then that General Albert Wedemeyer—returned from a presidential mission to the Far East—submitted to the President this warning: "The withdrawal of American military forces from Korea would result in the occupation of South Korea by either Soviet troops or, as seems more likely, by the Korean military units trained under Soviet auspices in North Korea."

That warning and his entire report were disregarded and suppressed by the Administration.

The terrible record of these years reaches its dramatic climax in a series of unforgettable scenes on Capitol Hill in June of 1949. By then the decision to complete withdrawal of American forces from Korea—despite menacing signs from the North—had been drawn up by the Department of State. The decision included the intention to ask Congress for aid to Korea to compensate for the withdrawal of American forces.

This brought questions from Congress. The Administration parade of civilian and military witnesses before the House Foreign Affairs Committee was headed by the Secretary of State. He and his aides faced a group of Republican congressmen both skeptical and fearful.

What followed was historic and decisive.

I beg you to listen carefully to the words that followed, for they shaped this nation's course from that date to this.

Listen, then:

First: Republican Congressman John Lodge of Connecticut asked: "[Do] you feel that the Korean Government is able to fill the vacuum caused by the withdrawal of the occupation forces?"

The Administration answered: "Definitely."

Second: A very different estimate of the risk involved came from Republican Congressman Walter Judd of Minnesota. He warned: "I think the thing necessary to give security to Korea at this stage of the game is the presence of a small American force and the knowledge (on the Soviet side) that attack upon it would bring trouble with us."

"I am convinced," Representative Judd continued, "that if we keep even a battalion there, they are not going to move. And if the battalion is not there"—listen now to his warning—"the chances are they will move within a year."

What a tragedy that the Administration shrugged off that so accurate warning!

Third: The Secretary of State was asked if he agreed that the South Koreans alone—and I quote—"will be able to defend themselves against any attack from the northern half of the country." To this the Secretary answered briskly: "We share the same view. Yes, sir."

Rarely in congressional testimony has so much misinformation been compressed so efficiently into so few words.

Fourth: Republican Congressman Lodge had an incisive comment on all this. "That," he said, "is wishful thinking. . . . I am afraid it confesses a kind of fundamental isolationism that exists in certain branches of the Government, which I think is a very dangerous pattern. I think the presence of our troops there is a tremendous deterrent to the Russians."

Finally: This remarkable scene of the summer of 1949 ends with a memorable document. The minority report of five Republican members of the House Foreign Affairs Committee on July 26, 1949, submitted this solemn warning.

Listen to it.

"It is reliably reported that Soviet troops, attached to the North Korean puppet armies, are in position of command as well as acting as advisers. . . . This development may well presage the launching of a full-scale military drive across the Thirty-eighth Parallel.

"Our forces . . . have been withdrawn from South Korea at the very instant when logic and common sense both demanded no retreat from the realities of the situation."

The report continues: "Already along the Thirty-eighth Parallel aggression is speaking with the too-familiar voices of howitzers and cannons. Our position is untenable and indefensible.

"The House should be aware of these facts."

These words of eloquent, reasoned warning were spoken eleven months before the Korean war broke.

Behind these words was a fervent, desperate appeal. That appeal was addressed to the Administration. It begged at least some firm statement of American intention that might deter the foreseen attack.

What was the Administration answer to that appeal?

The first answer was silence—stubborn, sullen silence for six months.

Then, suddenly, came speech—a high government official at long last speaking out on Asia. It was now January of 1950. What did he say? He said, "The United States Government will not provide military aid or advice to Chinese forces on Formosa."

Then, one week later, the Secretary of State announced his famous "defense perimeter"—publicly advising our enemies that, so far as nations outside this perimeter were concerned, "no person can guarantee these areas against military attack." Under these circumstances, it was cold comfort to the nations outside this perimeter to be reminded that they could appeal to the United Nations.

These nations, of course, included Korea. The armies of communism, thus informed, began their big build-up. Six months later they were ready to strike across the Thirty-eighth Parallel. They struck on June 25, 1950.

On that day, the record of political and diplomatic failure of this Administration was completed and sealed.

The responsibility for this record cannot be dodged or evaded. Even if not a single Republican leader had warned so clearly against the coming disaster, the responsibility for the fateful political decisions would still rest wholly with the men charged with making those decisions—in the Department of State and in the White House. They cannot escape that responsibility now or ever.

When the enemy struck, on that June day of 1950, what did America do? It did what it always has done in all its times of peril. It appealed to the heroism of its youth.

This appeal was utterly right and utterly inescapable. It was inescapable not only because this was the only way to defend the idea of collective freedom against savage aggression. That appeal was inescapable because there was now in the plight into which we had stumbled no other way to save honor and self-respect.

The answer to that appeal has been what any American knew it would be. It has been sheer valor—valor on all the Korean mountainsides that, each day, bear fresh scars of new graves.

Now—in this anxious autumn—from these heroic men there comes back an answering appeal. It is no whine, no whimpering plea. It is a question that addresses itself to simple reason. It asks: Where do we go from here? When comes the end? Is there an end?

These questions touch all of us. They demand truthful answers. Neither glib promises nor glib excuses will serve. They would be no better than the glib prophecies that brought us to this pass.

To these questions there are two false answers—both equally false. The first would be any answer that dishonesty pledged an end to war in Korea by any imminent, exact date. Such a pledge would brand its speaker as a deceiver.

The second and equally false answer declares that nothing can be done to speed a secure peace. It dares to tell us that we, the strongest nation in the history of freedom, can only wait—and wait—and wait. Such a statement brands its speaker as a defeatist.

My answer—candid and complete—is this:

The first task of a new Administration will be to review and reexamine every course of action open to us with one goal in view: To bring the Korean war to an early, and honorable end. That is my pledge to the American people.

For this task a wholly new Administration is necessary. The reason for this is simple. The old Administration cannot be expected to repair what it failed to prevent.

Where will a new Administration begin?

It will begin with its President taking a simple, firm resolution. That resolution will be: To forgo the diversions of politics and to concentrate on the job of ending the Korean war—until that job is honorably done.

That job requires a personal trip to Korea.

I shall make that trip. Only in that way could I learn how best to serve the American people in the cause of peace.

I shall go to Korea.

That is my second pledge to the American people.

Carefully, then, this new Administration, unfettered by past decisions and inherited mistakes, can review every factor—military, political and psychological—to be mobilized in speeding a just peace.

Progress along at least two lines can instantly begin. We can—first—step up the program of training and arming the South Korean forces. Manifestly, under the circumstances of today, United Nations forces cannot abandon that unhappy land.

But just as troops of the Republic of Korea covet and deserve the honor of defending their frontiers, so should we give them maximum assistance to insure their ability to do so.

Then, United Nations forces in reserve positions and supporting roles would be assurance that disaster would not again strike.

We can—secondly—shape our psychological warfare program into a weapon capable of cracking the Communist front.

Beyond all this we must carefully weigh all interrelated courses of action. We will, of course, constantly confer with associated free nations of Asia and with the cooperating members of the United Nations. Thus we could bring into being a practical plan for world peace.

That is my third pledge to you.

As the next Administration goes to work for peace, we must be guided at every instant by that lesson I spoke of earlier. The vital lesson is this: To vacillate, to appease, to placate is only to invite war—vaster war—bloodier war. In the words of the late Senator [Arthur H.] Vandenberg, appeasement is not the road to peace; it is only surrender on the installment plan.

I will always reject appeasement.

And that is my fourth pledge to you.

A nation's foreign policy is a much graver matter than rustling papers and bustling conferences. It is much more than diplomatic decisions and trade treaties and military arrangements.

A foreign policy is the face and voice of a whole people. It is all that the world sees and hears and understands about a single nation. It expresses the character and the faith and the will of that nation. In this, a nation is like any individual of our personal acquaintance; the simplest gesture can betray hesitation or weakness, the merest inflection of voice can reveal doubt or fear.

It is in this deep sense that our foreign policy has faltered and failed.

For a democracy, a great election, such as this, signifies a most solemn trial. It is the time when—to the bewilderment of all tryants—the people sit in judgment upon the leaders. It is the time when these leaders are summoned before the bar of public decision. There they must give evidence both to justify their actions and explain their intentions.

In the great trial of this election, the judges—the people—must not be deceived into believing that the choice is between isolationism and internationalism. That is a debate of the dead past. The vast majority of Americans of both parties know that to keep their own nation free, they bear a majestic responsibility for freedom through all the world. As practical people, Americans also know the critical necessity of unimpaired access to raw materials on other continents for our own economic and military strength.

Today the choice—the real choice—lies between policies that assume that responsibility awkwardly and fearfully—and policies that accept that responsibility with sure purpose and firm will. The choice is between foresight and blindness, between doing and apologizing, between planning and improvising.

In rendering their verdict, the people must judge with courage and with wisdom. For—at this date—any faltering in America's leadership is a capital offense against freedom.

In this trial, my testimony, of a personal kind, is quite simple. A soldier all my life, I have enlisted in the greatest cause of my life—the cause of peace.

I do not believe it a presumption for me to call the effort of all who have enlisted with me—a crusade.

I use that word only to signify two facts. First: We are united and devoted to a just cause of the purest meaning to all humankind. Second: We know that—for all the might of our effort—victory can come only with the gift of God's help.

In this spirit—humble servants of a proud ideal—we do soberly say: This is a crusade.

NEW ADMINISTRATION

FAREWELL TO THE NATION [1]

HARRY S. TRUMAN [2]

President Harry S. Truman gave this farewell "fireside address" to the nation, from his desk in the White House on Thursday evening, January 15, 1953. It was carried over all major TV and radio networks.

Although several speech writers collaborated in the composition, it was essentially Truman's own. It was mainly the expansion of some fifteen pages of notes jotted down by the President on the Sunday preceding the broadcast.[3]

The tone is highly personal. \Beginning with familiar observations concerning the routine of the presidential duties, Truman moved into a summary and defense of his leading foreign policies and decisions. The language is simple and the running narrative engrossing. The delivery was more communicative and individual than was usually the case when Truman undertook to talk from a manuscript. All in all, it was one of Truman's best speeches of recent years.

Readers of the address, and those who saw or heard the performance, will again and again discuss the question of Truman's place in history. Was he to be closely identified with mink coats, the Missouri gang, the whistle-stop vituperative speeches, the ways of a domestic politician? Or was he the statesman who for eight difficult years bore his immense responsibilities in the world and did so with vast courage and good judgment? In the judgment of this critic, President Truman will measure up well as constructive statesman among the "better" American presidents. In that influence his oral communication, although accompanied by elements that are obviously mediocre, was an important factor in his eight years' leadership.

I am happy to have this opportunity to talk to you once more before I leave the White House.

Next Tuesday, General Eisenhower will be inaugurated as President of the United States. A short time after the new Presi-

---

[1] Text is from the Des Moines *Register*, January 16, 1953. For identical text see *Congressional Record*, 99:439-41, January 16, 1953.

[2] For biographical note, see Appendix.

[3] See report from the Des Moines *Register's* Washington Bureau, Friday, January 16, 1953.

dent takes his oath of office, I will be on the train going back home to Independence, Missouri. I will once again be a plain, private citizen of this republic.

That is as it should be. Inauguration day will be a great demonstration of our democratic process. I am glad to be a part of it—glad to wish General Eisenhower all possible success, as he begins his term—glad the whole world will have a chance to see how simply and how peacefully our American system transfers the vast power of the presidency from my hands to his. It is a good object lesson in democracy. I am proud of it. I know you are, too.

During the last two months, I have done my best to make this transfer an orderly one. I have talked with my successor on the affairs of the country, both foreign and domestic, and my cabinet officers have talked with their successors. I want to say that General Eisenhower and his associates have cooperated fully in this effort. Such an orderly transfer from one party to another has never taken place before in our history. I think a real precedent has been set.

In speaking to you tonight, I have no new revelations to make—no political statements —no policy announcements. There are simply a few things in my heart I want to say to you. I want to say good-by and thanks for your help. And I want to talk with you a little about what has happened since I became your President.

I am speaking to you from the room where I have worked since April 1945. This is the President's office in the west wing of the White House. And this is the desk where I have signed most of the papers that embodied the decisions I have made as President. It has been the desk of many presidents, and will be the desk of many more.

Since I became President, I have been to Europe, Mexico, Canada, Brazil, Puerto Rico and the Virgin Islands—Wake Island and Hawaii. I have visited almost every state in the union. I have traveled 135,000 miles by air, 77,000 by rail, and 17,000 by ship. But the mail always followed me, and wherever I happened to be, that's where the office of the President was.

The greatest part of the President's job is to make decisions —big ones and small ones, dozens of them almost every day. The papers may circulate around the government for a while but they finally reach this desk. And then, there's no place else for them to go. The President—whoever he is—has to decide.

He can't pass the buck to anybody. No one else can do the deciding for him. That's his job.

That's what I've been doing here in this room, for almost eight years now. And over in the main part of the White House, there's a study on the second floor—a room much like this one— where I have worked at night and early in the morning on the papers I couldn't get to at the office.

Of course, for more than three years, Mrs. Truman and I were not living in the White House. We were across the street in the Blair House. That was when the White House almost fell down on us and had to be rebuilt. I had a study over at the Blair House, too, but living in the Blair House was not as convenient as living in the White House.

The Secret Service wouldn't let me walk across the street, so I had to get in a car every morning to cross the street to the White House office, again at noon to go to the Blair House for lunch, again to go back to the office after lunch, and finally take an automobile at night to return to the Blair House. Fantastic, isn't it? But necessary, so my guards thought—and they are the bosses on such matters as that.

Now, of course, we're back in the White House. It is in very good condition, and General Eisenhower will be able to take up his residence in the house and work right here. That will be much more convenient for him, and I'm very glad the renovation job was all completed before his term began.

Your new President is taking office in quite different circumstances than when I became President eight years ago. On April 12, 1945, I had been presiding over the Senate in my capacity as Vice President. When the senate recessed about five o'clock in the afternoon, I walked over to the office of the Speaker of the House, Mr. [Sam] Rayburn, to discuss pending legislation.

As soon as I arrived, I was told that Mr. [Steve] Early, one of President Roosevelt's secretaries, wanted me to call. I reached Mr. Early, and he told me to come to the White House as quickly as possible, to enter by way of the Pennsylvania Avenue entrance, and come to Mrs. Roosevelt's study.

When I arrived, Mrs. Roosevelt told me the tragic news, and I felt the shock that all of you felt a little later—when the word came over the radio and appeared in the newspapers. President Roosevelt had died. I offered to do anything I could for Mrs. Roosevelt, and then I asked the Secretary of State to call the Cabinet together.

At 7:09 P.M. I was sworn in as President by Chief Justice Stone in the Cabinet room.

Things were happening fast in those days. The San Francisco Conference to organize the United Nations had been called for April 25. I was asked if that meeting would go forward. I announced that it would.

After attending President Roosevelt's funeral, I went to the hall of the House of Representatives and told a joint session of the Congress that I would carry on President Roosevelt's policies.

On May 7, Germany surrendered. The announcement was made on May 8, my sixty-first birthday.

Mr. Churchill called me shortly after that and wanted a meeting with me and Prime Minister Stalin of Russia. Later on, a meeting was agreed upon, and Churchill, Stalin, and I met at Potsdam in Germany.

Meanwhile, the first atomic explosion took place out in the New Mexico desert.

The war against Japan was still going on. I made the decision that the atomic bomb had to be used to end it. I made that decision in the conviction it would save hundreds of thousands of lives—Japanese as well as American. Japan surrendered, and we were faced with the huge problems of bringing the troops home and reconverting the economy from war to peace.

All these things happened within just a little over four months—from April to August, 1945. I tell you this to illustrate the tremendous scope of the work your President has to do.

All these emergencies and all the developments to meet them have required the President to put in long hours—usually seventeen hours a day, with no payment for overtime. I sign my name on the average six hundred times a day, see and talk to hundreds of people every month, shake hands with thousands every year, and still carry on the business of the largest going concern in the world.

There is no job like it on the face of the earth—in the power which is concentrated here at this desk, and in the responsibility and difficulty of the decisions.

I want all of you to realize how big a job, how hard a job, it is—not for my sake, because I am stepping out of it—but for the sake of my successor.

He needs the understanding and the help of every citizen. It is not enough for you to come out once every four years and vote for a candidate, and then go back home and say, "Well, I've done my part, now let the new President do the worrying." He can't do the job alone.

Regardless of your politics, whether you are Republican or Democrat, your fate is tied up with what is done here in this room.

The President is President of the whole country. We must all give him our support as citizens of the United States. He will have mine, and I want you to give him yours.

I suppose that history will remember my term in office as the years when the "cold war" began to overshadow our lives.

I have had hardly a day in office that has not been dominated by this all-embracing struggle—this conflict between those who love freedom and those who would lead the world back into slavery and darkness. And always in the background there has been the atomic bomb.

But when history says that my term of office saw the beginning of the "cold war," it will also say that in those eight years we have set the course that can win it. We have succeeded in carving out a new set of policies to attain peace—positive policies, policies of world leadership, policies that express faith in other free people.

We have averted World War III up to now, and we may already have succeeded in establishing conditions which can keep that war from happening as far ahead as man can see.

These are great and historic achievements that we can all be proud of. Think of the difference between our course now and our course thirty years ago. After the first World War, we withdrew from world affairs—we failed to act in concert with other peoples against aggression—we helped to kill the League of Nations—and we built up tariff barriers which strangled world trade.

This time, we avoided those mistakes. We helped to found and to sustain the United Nations. We have welded alliances that include the greater part of the free world. And we have gone ahead with other free countries to help build their economies and link us all together in a healthy world trade.

Think back for a moment to the 1930's and you will see the difference.

The Japanese moved into Manchuria, and free men did not act. The Fascists moved into Ethiopia, and we did not act. The Nazis marched into the Rhineland, into Austria, into Czechoslovakia, and free men were paralyzed for lack of strength and unity and will.

Think about those years of weakness and indecision, and World War II which was their evil result. Then think about the speed and courage and decisiveness with which we have moved against the Communist threat since World War II.

The first crisis came in 1945 and 1946, when the Soviet Union refused to honor its agreement to remove its troops from Iran. Members of my Cabinet came to me and asked if we were ready to take the risk that a firm stand involved. I replied that we were. So we took our stand—we made it clear to the Soviet Union that we expected them to honor their agreement—and the Soviet troops were withdrawn.

And then, in early 1947, the Soviet Union threatened Greece and Turkey. The British sent me a message saying they could no longer keep their forces in that area. Something had to be done at once, or the eastern Mediterranean would be taken over by the Communists.

On March 12, I went before the Congress and stated our determination to help the people of Greece and Turkey maintain their independence. Today, Greece is still free and independent; and Turkey is a bulwark of strength at a strategic corner of the world.

Then came the Marshall Plan which saved Europe, the heroic Berlin airlift, and our military aid programs.

We inaugurated the North Atlantic pact, the Rio pact binding the Western Hemisphere together, and the defense pacts with countries of the far Pacific.

Most important of all, we acted in Korea.

I was in Independence, Missouri, in June 1950, when Secretary Acheson telephoned me and gave me the news about the invasion of Korea. I told the Secretary to lay the matter at once before the United Nations, and I came on back to Washington.

Flying back over the flat lands of the Middle West and over the Appalachians that summer afternoon, I had a lot of time to think. I turned the problem over in my mind in many ways, but my thoughts kept coming back to the 1930's—to Manchuria —Ethiopia—the Rhineland—Austria—and finally to Munich.

Here was history repeating itself. Here was another probing action, another testing action. If we let the Republic of Korea go under, some other country would be next, and then another. And all the time, the courage and confidence of the free world would be ebbing away, just as it did in the 1930's. And the United Nations would go the way of the League of Nations.

When I reached Washington, I met immediately with the Secretary of State, the Secretary of Defense, and General Bradley, and the other civilian and military officials who had information and advice to help me decide what to do. We talked about the problems long and hard.

It was not easy to make the decision that sent American boys again into battle. I was a soldier in the First World War, and I know what a soldier goes through. I know well the anguish that mothers and fathers and families go through. So I knew what was ahead if we acted in Korea.

But after all this was said, we realized that the issue was whether there would be fighting in a limited area now or on a much larger scale later on—whether there would be some casualties now or many more casualties later.

So a decision was reached—the decision I believe was the most important in my time as President.

In the days that followed, the most heartening fact was that the American people clearly agreed with the decision.

And in Korea, our men are fighting as valiantly as Americans have ever fought—because they know they are fighting in the same cause of freedom in which Americans have stood ever since the beginning of the Republic.

Where free men had failed the test before, this time we met the test.

We met it firmly. We met it successfully. The aggression has been repelled. The Communists have seen their hopes of easy conquest go down the drain.

The determination of free people to defend themselves has been made clear to the Kremlin.

As I have thought about our world-wide struggle with the Communists these past eight years—day in and day out—I have never once doubted that you, the people of our country, have the will to do what is necessary to win this terrible fight against communism. Because I have been sure of that, I have been able to make necessary decisions even though they called for sacrifices by all of us. And I have not been wrong in my judgment of the American people.

That same assurance of our people's determination will be General Eisenhower's greatest source of strength in carrying on this struggle.

Now, once in a while, I get a letter from some impatient person asking, "Why don't we get it over with? Why don't we issue an ultimatum, make all-out war, drop the atomic bomb?"

For most Americans, the answer is quite simple: We are not made that way. We are a moral people. Peace is our goal, and justice and freedom. We cannot, of our own free will, violate the very principles that we are striving to defend. The whole purpose of what we are doing is to prevent World War III. Starting a war is no way to make peace.

But if anyone still thinks that just this once, bad means can bring good ends, then let me remind you of this: We are living in the eighth year of the atomic age. We are not the only nation that is learning to unleash the power of the atom. A third world war might dig the grave not only of our Communist opponents but also of our own society, our world as well as theirs.

Starting an atomic war is totally unthinkable for rational men.

Then, some of you may ask, when and how will the "cold war" ever end? I think I can answer that simply. The Communist world has great resources, and it looks strong. But there is a fatal flaw in their society. Theirs is a godless system, a system of slavery; there is no freedom in it, no consent. The Iron Curtain, the secret police, the constant purges, all these are symptoms of a great basic weakness—the rulers' fear of their own people.

In the long run, the strength of our free society, and our ideals, will prevail over a system that has respect for neither God nor man.

Last week, in my State of the Union message to the Congress —and I hope you will all take time to read it—I explained how I think we will finally win through.

As the free world grows stronger, more united, more attractive to men on both sides of the Iron Curtain—and as the Soviet hopes for easy expansion are blocked—then there will have to come a time of change in the Soviet world. Nobody can say for sure when that is going to be, or exactly how it will come about, whether by revolution, or trouble in the satellite states, or by a change inside the Kremlin.

Whether the Communist rulers shift their policies of their own free will—or whether the change comes about in some other way—I have not a doubt in the world that a change will occur.

I have a deep and abiding faith in the destiny of free men. With patience and courage, we shall some day move on into a new era—a wonderful golden age—an age when we can use the peaceful tools that science has forged for us to do away with poverty and human misery everywhere on earth.

Think what can be done, once our capital, our skills, our science—most of all atomic energy—can be released from the tasks of defense and turned wholly to peaceful purposes all around the world.

There is no end to what can be done.

I can't help but dream out loud a little here.

The Tigris and Euphrates Valley can be made to bloom as it did in the times of Babylon and Nineveh. Israel can be made the country of milk and honey as it was in the time of Joshua.

There is a plateau in Ethiopia some six to eight thousand feet high, that has sixty-five thousand square miles of land just exactly like the corn belt in northern Illinois. Enough food can be raised there to feed a hundred million people.

There are places in South America—places in Colombia and Venezuela and Brazil—just like that plateau in Ethiopia—places where food could be raised for millions of people.

These things can be done, and they are self-liquidating projects. If we can get peace and safety in the world under the United Nations, the developments will come so fast we will not recognize the world in which we now live.

This is our dream of the future—our picture of the world we hope to have when the Communist threat is overcome.

I've talked a lot tonight about the menace of communism— and our fight against it—because that is the overriding issue of our time. But there are some other things we've done that history will record. One of them is that we in America have learned how to attain real prosperity for our people.

We have 62.5 million people at work. Businessmen, farmers, laborers, white collar people, all have better incomes and more of the good things of life than ever before in the history of the world.

There hasn't been a failure of an insured bank in nearly nine years. No depositor has lost a cent in that period.

And the income of our people has been fairly distributed, perhaps more so than at any time in recent history.

We have made progress in spreading the blessings of American life to all of our people. There has been a tremendous awakening of the American conscience on the great issues of civil rights—equal economic opportunities, equal rights of citizenship, and equal educational opportunities for all our people, whatever their race or religion or status of birth.

So, as I empty the drawers of this desk, and as Mrs. Truman and I leave the White House, we have no regret. We feel we have done our best in the public service. I hope and believe we have contributed to the welfare of this nation and to the peace of the world.

When Franklin Roosevelt died, I felt there must be a million men better qualified than I to take up the presidential task. But the work was mine to do, and I had to do it. I have tried to give it everything that was in me.

Through all of it, through all the years that I have worked here in this room, I have been well aware I did not really work alone—that you were working with me.

No President could ever hope to lead our country, or to sustain the burdens of this office, save as the people helped with their support. I have had that help—you have given me that support—on all our great essential undertakings to build the free world's strength and keep the peace.

Those are the big things. Those are the things we have done together.

For that I shall be grateful, always.

And now, the time has come for me to say good night and— God bless you all.

INAUGURAL ADDRESS [4]

DWIGHT D. EISENHOWER [5]

President Dwight D. Eisenhower gave this inaugural address on Tuesday, January 20, 1953, immediately after Chief Justice Fred M. Vinson had administered the oath of office at 12:32, in the presence of some hundred thousand spectators in the plaza fronting the United States Capitol. The weather, in contrast to that of several previous inaugural occasions, was mild and even sunshiny. The ceremonies and the four-hour-long parade afterward were broadcast and televised by the major networks. It was the first such occasion to be viewed in detail by millions of Americans throughout the land. It marked a new introduction of the rank and file to political history and no doubt brought the 160 million citizens in much closer relation to their central government than had hitherto been possible.

The Republicans, out of office for twenty years, celebrated with proper demonstration. The inaugural parade, for example, was the longest and noisiest in inaugural history. The president reviewed the marchers for more than four hours "into the dark of the night."

The message itself, prefaced by the President's private prayer, was reverently received but with little applause. The radio commentators and press, including overseas opinion, rated the speech as "excellent" in its note of international unity and purpose and in its appeal for "this community of fraternal trust and common purpose." Significant was its complete commitment by the United States to internationalism. The message appealed for faith—in human dignity, freedom, and ethical precepts of the world's great religions.

Highly didactic and no doubt reassuring to the millions over the globe who listened, it was not highly original in its phrasing or ideas. It fell just short of the character of Lincoln's second inaugural of Woodrow Wilson's "new freedom" address of 1913.[6]

My friends, before I begin the expression of those thoughts which I deem appropriate to this moment, would you permit me the privilege of uttering a little private prayer of my own, and I ask that you bow your heads.

[4] Text supplied by the White House. See also *Congressional Record*, 99: 465-66, January 20, 1953 (daily edition).

[5] For biographical note, see Appendix.

[6] *Cf.* F. D. Roosevelt's Fourth Inaugural Address, *Representative American Speeches: 1944-45*, p 153-156.

Almighty God, as we stand here, at this moment, my future associates in the executive branch of government join me in beseeching that Thou wilt make full and complete our dedication to the service of the people in this throng and their fellow citizens everywhere. Give us, we pray, the power to discern clearly right from wrong and allow all our words and actions to be governed thereby and by the laws of this land.

Especially we pray that our concern shall be for all the people—regardless of station, race, or calling. May cooperation be permitted and be the mutual aim of those who, under the concepts of our Constitution, hold to differing political beliefs, so that all may work for the good of our beloved country and for Thy glory. Amen.

My fellow citizens, the world and we have passed the midway point of a century of continuing challenge. We sense with all our faculties that forces of good and evil are massed and armed and opposed as rarely before in history.

This fact defines the meaning of this day. We are summoned, by this honored and historic ceremony, to witness more than the act of one citizen swearing his oath of service, in the presence of his God. We are called, as a people, to give testimony, in the sight of the world, to our faith that the future shall belong to the free.

Since this century's beginning, a time of tempest has seemed to come upon the continents of the earth. Masses of Asia have wakened to strike off shackles of the past. Great nations of Europe have waged their bloodiest wars. Thrones have toppled and their vast empires have disappeared. New nations have been born.

For our own country, it has been a time of recurring trial. We have grown in power and in responsibility. We have passed through the anxieties of depression and of war to a summit unmatched in man's history. Seeking to secure peace in the world, we have had to fight through the forests of the Argonne to the shores of Iwo Jima, and to the mountain peaks of Korea.

In the swift rush of great events, we find ourselves groping to know the full sense and meaning of the times in which we live. In our quest of understanding, we beseech God's guidance. We summon all our knowledge of the past and we scan all signs of the future. We bring all our wit and will to meet the question: How far have we come in man's long pilgrimage from darkness toward light? Are we nearing the light—a day of freedom and of peace for all mankind? Or are the shadows of another night closing in upon us?

Great as are the preoccupations absorbing us at home, concerned as we are with matters that deeply affect our livelihood today and our vision of the future, each of these domestic problems is dwarfed by, and often even created by, this question that involves all human kind.

This trial comes at a moment when man's power to achieve good or to inflict evil surpasses the brightest hopes and the sharpest fears of all ages. We can turn rivers in their courses, level mountains to the plains. Ocean and land and sky are avenues for our colossal commerce. Disease diminishes and life lengthens.

Yet, the promise of this life is imperiled by the very genius that has made it possible. Nations amass wealth. Labor sweats to create—and turns out devices to level not only mountains but also cities. Science seems ready to confer upon us, as its final gift, the power to erase human life from the earth.

At such a time in history, we who are free must proclaim anew our faith.

This faith is the abiding creed of our fathers. It is our faith in the deathless dignity of man, governed by eternal moral and natural laws. This faith defines our full view of life. It establishes, beyond debate, those gifts of the Creator that are man's inalienable rights, and that make all men equal in His sight.

In the light of this equality, we know that the virtues most cherished by free people—love of truth, pride of work, devotion to country—all are treasures equally precious in the lives of the most humble and of the most exalted. The men who mine coal and fire furnaces and balance ledgers and turn lathes and pick cotton and heal the sick and plant corn, all serve as proudly, and as profitably, for America as the statesmen who draft treaties or the legislators who enact laws.

This faith rules our whole way of life. It decrees that we, the people, elect leaders not to rule but to serve. It asserts that we have the right to choice of our own work and to the reward of our own toil. It inspires the initiative that makes our productivity the wonder of the world. And it warns that any man who seeks to deny equality in all his brothers betrays the spirit of the free and invites the mockery of the tyrant.

It is because we, all of us, hold to these principles that the political changes accomplished this day do not imply turbulence, upheaval, or disorder. Rather this change expresses a purpose of strengthening our dedication and devotion to the precepts of our founding documents, a conscious renewal of faith in our country and in the watchfulness of a divine providence.

The enemies of this faith know no god but force, no devotion but its use. They tutor men in treason. They feed upon the hunger of others. Whatever defies them, they torture, especially the truth.

Here, then, is joined no pallid argument between slightly differing philosophies. This conflict strikes directly at the faith of our fathers and the lives of our sons. No principle or treasure that we hold, from the spiritual knowledge of our free schools and churches to the creative magic of free labor and capital, nothing lies safely beyond the reach of the struggle.

Freedom is pitted against slavery; light against dark.

The faith we hold belongs not to us alone but to the free of all the world. This common bond binds the grower of rice in Burma and the planter of wheat in Iowa, the shepherd in southern Italy and the mountaineer in the Andes. It confers a common dignity upon the French soldier who dies in Indo-China, the British soldier killed in Malaya, the American life given in Korea.

We know, beyond this, that we are linked to all free peoples not merely by a noble idea but by a simple need. No free people can for long cling to any privilege or enjoy any safety in economic solitude. For all our own material might, even we need markets in the world for the surpluses of our farms and of our factories. Equally, we need for these same farms and factories vital materials and products of distant lands.

This basic law of interdependence, so manifest in the commerce of peace, applies with thousandfold intensity in the event of war. So are we persuaded by necessity and by belief that the strength of all free peoples lies in unity, their danger in discord. To produce this unity, to meet the challenge of our time, destiny has laid upon our country the responsibility of the free world's leadership.

So it is proper that we assure our friends once again that, in the discharge of this responsibility, we Americans know and observe the difference between world leadership and imperialism; between firmness and truculence; between a thoughtfully calculated goal and spasmodic reaction to the stimulus of emergencies.

We wish our friends the world over to know this above all: We face the threat—not with dread and confusion—but with confidence and conviction. We feel this moral strength because we know that we are not helpless prisoners of history. We are free men. We shall remain free, never to be proven guilty of the one capital offense against freedom, a lack of staunch faith. In pleading our just cause before the bar of history and in pressing our labor for world peace, we shall be guided by certain fixed principles.

These principles are:

(1) Abhorring war as a chosen way to balk the purpose of those who threaten us, we hold it to be the first task of statesmanship to develop the strength that will deter the forces of aggression and promote the conditions of peace. For, as it must be the supreme purpose of all free men, so it must be the dedication of their leaders, to save humanity from preying upon itself.

In light of this principle, we stand ready to engage with any and all others in joint effort to remove the causes of mutual fear and distrust among nations, and so to make possible drastic reduction of armaments.

The sole requisites for undertaking such effort are that—in their purpose—they are aimed logically and honestly toward secure peace for all; and that—in their result—they provide methods by which every participating nation will prove good faith in carrying out its pledge.

(2) Realizing that common sense and common decency alike dictate the futility of appeasement, we shall never try to placate an aggressor by the false and wicked bargain of trading honor for security. For in the final choice a soldier's pack is not so heavy a burden as a prisoner's chains.

(3) Knowing that only a United States that is strong and immensely productive can help defend freedom in our world, we view our nation's strength and security as a trust upon which rests the hope of free men everywhere. It is the firm duty of each of our free citizens and of every free citizen everywhere to place the cause of his country before the comfort and convenience of himself.

(4) Honoring the identity and heritage of each nation of the world, we shall never use our strength to try to impress upon another people our own cherished political and economic institutions.

(5) Assessing realistically the needs and capacities of proven friends of freedom, we shall strive to help them to achieve their own security and well-being. Likewise, we shall count upon them to assume, within the limits of their resources, their full and just burdens in the common defense of freedom.

(6) Recognizing economic health as an indispensable basis of military strength and the free world's peace, we shall strive to foster everywhere, and to practice ourselves, policies that encourage productivity and profitable trade. For the impoverishment of any single people in the world means danger to the well-being of all other peoples.

(7) Appreciating that economic need, military security and political wisdom combine to suggest regional groupings of free peoples, we hope, within the framework of the United Nations, to help strengthen such special bonds the world over.

The nature of these ties must vary with the different problems of different areas. In the Western Hemisphere, we enthusiastically join with all our neighbors in the work of perfecting a community of fraternal trust and common purpose.

In Europe, we ask that enlightened and inspired leaders of the Western nations strive with renewed vigor to make the unity of their peoples a reality. Only as free Europe unitedly marshals its strength can it effectively safeguard, even with our help, its spiritual and cultural heritages.

(8) Conceiving the defense of freedom, like freedom itself, to be one and indivisible, we hold all continents and peoples in equal regard and honor. We reject any insinuation that one race or another, one people or another, is in any sense inferior or expendable.

(9) Respecting the United Nations as the living sign of all people's hope for peace, we shall strive to make it not merely an eloquent symbol but an effective force. And in our quest of honorable peace, we shall neither compromise, nor tire, nor ever cease.

By these rules of conduct, we hope to be known to all peoples.

By their observance, an earth of peace may become not a vision but a fact.

This hope—this supreme aspiration—must rule the way we live.

We must be ready to dare all for our country. For history does not long entrust the care of freedom to the weak or the timid. We must acquire proficiency in defense and display stamina in purpose.

We must be willing, individually, and as a nation, to accept whatever sacrifices may be required of us. A people that values its privileges above its principles soon loses both.

These basic precepts are not lofty abstractions, far removed from matters of daily living. They are laws of spiritual strength that generate and define our material strength. Patriotism means equipped forces and a prepared citizenry. Moral stamina means more energy and more productivity, on the farm and in the factory. Love of liberty means the guarding of every resource that makes freedom possible—from the sanctity of our families and the wealth of our soil to the genius of our scientists.

So each citizen plays an indispensable role. The productivity of our heads, our hands, and our hearts is the source of all the strength we can command, for both the enrichment of our lives and the winning of peace.

No person, no home, no community can be beyond the reach of this call. We are summoned to act in wisdom and in conscience; to work with industry, to teach with persuasion, to preach with conviction, to weigh our every deed with care and with compassion. For this truth must be clear before us: Whatever America hopes to bring to pass in the world must first come to pass in the heart of America.

The peace we seek, then, is nothing less than the practice and the fulfillment of our whole faith, among ourselves and in our dealings with others. It signifies more than stilling the guns, easing the sorrow, of war.

More than an escape from death, it is a way of life.

More than a haven for the weary, it is a hope for the brave.

This is the hope that beckons us onward in this century of trial. This is the work that awaits us all, to be done with bravery, with charity, and with prayer to Almighty God. [Great applause]

NATIONAL IDEALS

THE PREPARATION OF CITIZENS
FOR THEIR POLITICAL DUTIES [1]

LEARNED HAND [2]

Judge Learned Hand gave this address at Albany, New York, on October 24, 1952, before a state-wide gathering of some six hundred education officials attending the eighty-sixth convocation of the Board of Regents of the University of the State of New York.

The Judge's theme was the education of citizens as a preparation for their political duties. His position was that such education must in the long run depend upon education in the humanities—history, literature, philosophy, and the arts—"essential to political wisdom." In view of the current drift toward scientific education and away from classical studies, his emphasis was significant.

His thinking and language were strikingly original, in true form with his reasoning and expression in a long line of judicial writings and speeches. (In 1950 he had written the United States Circuit Court of Appeals opinion affirming the conviction of eleven top Communists in this country.)

His delivery was measured, but vigorous and lively. At all points he was communicative in spite of his adherence to the manuscript.

The Board of Regents conferred the honorary degree of Doctor of Laws on the Judge.[3]

Chancellor Myers, Regents of the University, Ladies and Gentlemen:

The honor which the University of the State confers upon me today is doubly grateful: it is one that all would crave, and in my own case it has an especial personal value; for I was born in a house only a few rods from the building in which we now are, and I lived there for over thirty years. I can remember

[1] The text and permission for this reprint given through the courtesy of Judge Hand. The speech was reprinted in the *Saturday Review*, 35:9-10, November 22, 1952, and in *Vital Speeches of the Day*, 19:173-76, January 1, 1953.

[2] For biographical note, see Appendix.

[3] For further comment on Judge Hand as speaker, see "We Seek Liberty," in *Representative American Speeches: 1943-44*, p254-57.

how, as a little boy, in the early morning I used to hear all the chisels begin together to chip the stones that were to be used in building the Capitol and how it seemed to me that that sound and the construction of that building were part of the permanent order of things and would always go on. Now, will you forgive me, if towards the close of a long life I lapse into a sentimental mood, as I reflect that an old man has been called back to the same spot where he took his first breath to be told that he has deserved well of his state during the intervening years. My father was born in New York, my grandfather lived in it all his professional life; they were loyal citizens of their state, and I like to fancy that their shades would join in my satisfaction at this evidence of your approval.

The theme today is education, as to which you, the Regents of the University, have an overarching superintendence. What I have to say will be directed towards one aspect of your responsibility: the preparation of citizens for their political duties. I shall argue that the "humanities," instead of being regarded only as a solace, a refuge, and an enrichment of the individual—as indeed they are—are also an essential factor in training him to perform his duties in a democratic society, as important even as acquaintance with the persons and the current events on which he is called upon to pass. The gifted men who contrived that great compromise, the Constitution of the United States, and secured its ratification by a society which might very probably have repudiated it upon a referendum, were well aware of the dangers which surrounded a totalitarian government, as well when power was lodged in the people at large, as when it rested in one man, or in an aristocracy. Indeed, some of the ablest of them, Hamilton for example, did not believe that any society could endure in which the voters had uncontrolled authority, even though the suffrage was as limited as it then was; and the experience of France in the next ten years seemed to them a demonstration that they had been right. The compunctions that all felt, including the people at large, were the reason why so many of the states made the first ten amendments practically a condition upon ratification, and they were all at once added, as you know. It is not important here whether it was from the outset inevitable that the word of the Supreme Court should be final as to what the Amendments meant; but it is important that they, and in particular the First and Fifth, contained hallowed phrases which thoughtful people at the end of the eighteenth century usually believed to embody mandates that either were of divine origin, or could be deduced from the inherent nature of man in society. Against these mandates no statute should prevail, and the Amendments, so far as they embodied them, were, strictly speaking, redundant. Moreover, it would not be true to say that this belief is not still widely held; indeed, one of the striking political agitations of the present is the recrudescence of the notion of "Natural Law" after its general repudiation by English-speaking lawyers in the nineteenth century. We are even assured that those who do not share it are "materialists" and amoral upholders of the doctrine that might makes right.

Most parts of the Constitution are specific enough to be treated like other legal commands; when we have to decide their meaning, we can proceed just as in the case of a dispute over the meaning of a statute; we look to their history and their setting with confidence that these will disclose their purpose. And that also applies to a large part of the Amendments themselves. For instance, no general cultural background is needed to reach a right opinion as to whether a statute has infringed the provision that the accused must be tried in the district where the crime was committed, or that he must be "confronted" by "the witnesses against him." But the situation is quite different when we are dealing with the broad clauses on which the conduct of a free society must in the end depend. What is "freedom of speech and of the press"; what is the "establishment of religion and the free exercise thereof"; what are "unreasonable searches," "due process of law," and "equal protection of the law": all these are left wholly undefined and cannot be effectively determined without some acquaintance with what men in the past have thought and felt to be their most precious interests. Indeed, these fundamental canons are not jural concepts at all, in the ordinary sense; and in application they turn out to be no more than admonitions of moderation, as appears from the varying and contradictory interpretations that the judges themselves find it necessary to put upon them. Nor can we leave to courts the responsibility of construing and so of enforcing them, for the powers of courts are too limited to reach the more controversial questions that arise under them. For, as you know, courts will not intervene—or at least they constantly avow that they should not—unless the action challenged infringes the Constitution beyond any fair dispute. While there are any plausible arguments in support of a measure, they must abstain; and so it results that in much the larger part of such controversies it is the voters, speaking through their delegates, who have the final word and the final responsibility; and that in the end it is they and they alone, who can and will preserve our liberties, if preserved they are to be. For their guidance there are no vade mecums, no handbooks, no manuals; they must depend upon such enlightenment as they can muster from within, and upon their conscience, so far as they have one. That enlightenment and that conscience they may indeed find in divine revelation; but when they do, they tap sources that I am not qualified to discuss; not any better qualified that I am to discuss what doctrines are inherent in the nature of man in society. I know of none of either sort, nor can I find direction from those who profess to know. It is because I am shorn of such resort that, to me at any rate, there appears to be no escape in each situation from balancing the conflicting interests at stake with as detached a temper as we can achieve.

A constitution, a statute, a regulation, a rule—in short, a "law" of any kind—is at once a prophecy and a choice. It is a prophecy, because it attempts to forecast what will be its effects: whom it will benefit and in what ways; on whom its impact will prove a burden; how much friction and discontent will arise from the adjustments that conformity to it will require; how completely it can be enforced; what enforcement will cost; how far it will interfere with other projects or existing activities; and in general, the whole manifold of its indirect consequences. A thoroughgoing and dependable knowledge of these is obviously impossible. For example, although we can anticipate with some degree of assurance who will pay a steeply graded income tax and in what amounts, there is no way to tell what its indirect effects will be: what activities of the taxpayers in the higher brackets it will depress; if they do not work so hard, in what way they will occupy their newly acquired leisure; how any new activities they may substitute will affect others; whether this will be offset by a loss of the mellowed maturity and the wisdom of those who withdraw. Such prophecies infest law of every sort, the more deeply as it is far reaching; and it is an illusion to suppose that there are formulas or statistics that will help in making them. They can rest upon no more than enlightened guesses; but these are likely to be successful as they are made by those whose horizons have been widened, and whose outlook has been clarified, by knowledge of what men have striven to do, and how far their hopes and fears have been realized. There is no substitute for an open mind, enriched by reading and the arts.

So much for what I have called the element of prophecy; refractory as it is, at least it depends only upon facts, however inaccessible. There remains the much more difficult element of choice. In such inquiries, as I have said, I see no escape from a calculus of, and balance between, the group interests—that is, the desires and values—whose conflict the measure under consideration is an attempt to adjust. But desires and values are not quantitatively measurable, for they seldom have any common constituents, and without these they cannot be objectively compared. On the other hand, an individual has the necessary means in his own case, for, although his personal desires and values are absolute, irreducible and undeducible, and have just that authority which he feels them to have, he has as authoritative a competence to compare them and to prefer one to another, as he has to appraise them separately. Thus, although such preferences are themselves as final as the desires and values, it would be easy to choose between the desires and values of conflicting social groups, if we could safely impute to them our own preferences. But by what right can we do so; and, if we cannot, what other means of vicarious choice have we? I submit that we have none except in so far as we can imaginatively project ourselves into the position of the groups between which we must choose. Surely I need not dilate upon how hard it is to do that. Even in our own affairs how often have we tried to anticipate how we shall feel on a future occasion, only to be surprised by the unexpected difference, when it comes to pass. And if it is hard to foreshadow our own feelings, how much harder is it to do so for others? It is not enough to be personally detached, although that is of course a condition; we must also acquire a capacity for an informed sympathy with and understanding of, the desires and the values of others; and that, I submit, only those have any chance of attaining whose experience is supplemented by some acquaintance, the wider the better, with what others have thought and felt in circumstances as near as possible to those of the groups in question.

I dare hope that it may now begin to be clearer why I am arguing that an education which includes the "humanities" is essential to political wisdom. By "humanities" I especially mean history; but close beside history and of almost, if not quite, equal importance are letters, poetry, philosophy, the plastic arts and music. Most of the issues that mankind sets out to settle, it never does settle. They are not solved, because, as I have just tried to say, they are incapable of solution properly speaking, being concerned with incommensurables. At any rate, even if that be not always true, the opposing parties seldom do agree upon a solution; and the dispute fades into the past unsolved, though perhaps it may be renewed as history and fought over again. It disappears because it is replaced by some compromise that, although not wholly acceptable to either side, offers a tolerable substitute for victory; and he who would find the substitute needs an endowment as rich as possible in experience, an experience which makes the heart generous and provides his mind with an understanding of the hearts of others. The great moderates of history were more often than not men of that sort, steeped, like Montaigne and Erasmus, in knowledge of the past. Let me quote from one of these, our own Franklin. After long, and at times bitter, controversy the final draft of the Constitution was accepted on Saturday, September 12, and was sent to be engrossed over the weekend. Nevertheless, there was still doubt about what might happen on Monday when the delegates were to sign. On Sunday Franklin wrote out a statement which Wilson read for him the next day. It is too long to quote *in extenso,* but I cannot forbear a sentence or two, so appropriate is it to what I am trying to say.

> I agree to this constitution with all its faults, if they are such, because I think a general government necessary for us and there is no form of government but what may be a blessing to the people if well administered, and believe further that this is likely to be well administered for a course of years, and can only end in despotism, as other forms have done before it, when the people shall have become so corrupted as to need despotic government, being incapable of any other. I doubt too whether any other convention we can obtain may be able to make a better constitution. For when you assemble a number of men to have the advantage of their joint wisdom, you inevitably assemble with those men all their prejudices, their passions, their errors of opinion, their local interests and their selfish views. From such an assembly can a perfect production be expected? . . . Thus, I consent Sir, to this constitution because I expect no better, and because I am not sure it is not the best.

Out of such a temper alone can come any political success which will not leave behind rancor and vindictiveness that is likely so deeply to infect its benefits as to make victory not worth while; and it is a temper best bred in those who have at least what I like to call a bowing acquaintance with the "humanities." For these are fitted to admonish us how tentative and provisional are our attainments, intellectual and moral; and how often the deepest convictions of one generation are the rejects of the next. That does not indeed deny the possibility that, as time goes on, we shall accumulate some body of valid conclusions; but it does mean that these we can achieve only by accumulation; that wisdom is to be gained only as we stand upon the shoulders of those who have gone before. Just as in science we cannot advance except as we take over what we inherit, so in statecraft no generation can safely start at scratch. The subject matter of science is recorded observation of the external world; the subject matter of the statecraft is the soul of man, and of that too there are records —the records I am talking about today. The imagination can be purged and the judgment ripened only by an awareness of the slow, hesitant, wayward course of human life, its failures, its successes, but its indomitable will to endure.

I cannot but think that we of this generation are politically in especial need of such education. Our nation is embarked upon a venture, as yet unproved; we have set our hopes upon a community in which men shall be given unchecked control of their own lives. That community is in peril; it is invaded from within, it is threatened from without; it faces a test which it may fail to pass. The choice is ours whether, when we hear the pipes of Pan, we shall stampede like a frightened flock, forgetting all those professions on which we have claimed to rest our polity. God knows, there is risk in refusing to act till the facts are all in; but is there not greater risk in abandoning the conditions of all rational inquiry? Risk for risk, for myself I had rather take my chance that some traitors will escape detection than spread abroad a spirit of general suspicion and distrust, which accepts rumor and gossip in place of undismayed and unintimidated inquiry. I believe that that community is already in process of dissolution where each man begins to eye his neighbor as a possible enemy, where nonconformity with the accepted creed, political as well as religious, is a mark of disaffection; where denunciation, without specification or backing, takes the place of evidence; where orthodoxy chokes freedom of dissent; where faith in the eventual supremacy of reason has become so timid that we dare not enter our convictions in the open lists to win or lose. Such fears as these are a solvent which can eat out the cement that binds the stones together; they may in the end subject us to a despotism as evil as any that we dread; and they can be allayed only in so far as we refuse to proceed on suspicion, and trust one another until we have tangible ground for misgiving. The mutual confidence on which all else depends can be maintained only by an open mind and a brave reliance upon free discussion. I do not say that these will suffice; who knows but we may be on a slope which leads down to aboriginal savagery. But of this I am sure: If we are to escape, we must not yield a foot upon demanding a fair field, and an honest race, to all ideas. "Blame not before thou hast examined; understand first and then rebuke. Answer not before thou hast heard; interrupt not in the midst of speech." Those words were written nearly two thousand years ago; they came out of an experience already long, and refined in the fires of passion and conflict; they are the product of a wisdom, bought by ages of bitter trial; and by that wisdom alone shall we be saved, we, who boast ourselves to be the apostles of a faith in the eventual triumph of wisdom. Listen also to these as ancient words that tell of the excellence of wisdom. "There is in her a spirit quick of understanding, holy, alone in kind, manifold, subtil, freely moving, clear in utterance, unpolluted, distinct, unharmed, loving what is good, keen, unhindered, beneficent, loving toward man, steadfast, sure, free from care, all-powerful, all-surveying, and penetrating through all spirits that are quick of understanding, pure, most subtil. . . . And if a man longeth even for much experience, he knoweth the things of old, and divineth the things to come; he understandeth subtilities of speeches and interpretations of dark sayings; he forseeth signs and wonders, and the issues of seasons and times. I determined therefore to take her unto me to live with me, knowing that she is one who would give me good thoughts for counsel, and encourage me in cares and griefs. . . . For she knoweth all things and hath understanding thereof; and in my doing she shall guide me in the ways of soberness, and she shall guard me in her glory. And so shall my works be acceptable, and I shall judge the people righteously, and shall be worthy of my Father's throne."

DOMESTIC ECONOMIC POLICIES

THE FREE WORLD CAN'T TRADE
ON A ONE-WAY STREET [1]

HENRY FORD II [2]

Henry Ford II, president of the Ford Motor Company, gave this address at the annual winter meeting of the Inland Daily Press Association, in Chicago, Illinois, on February 17, 1953.

The address was immediately hailed as an important one and resulted in considerable favorable comment in the press. It turned out to be as able a performance as Mr. Ford's historic speech on January 9, 1946, when this young executive had expounded the problem of "human relations in industrial production." One leading industrialist had pronounced it as "the best speech I've heard in ten years." G. F. Addes, Secretary-Treasurer of the United Automobile Workers, had also hailed Ford as "one of the greatest industrial statesmen of the auto industry." Ford's leadership on the platform and off during the years since 1946 had borne out these earlier estimates.

In the Chicago address, the speaker logically analyzed the issue of "trade, not aid." The successive steps of establishing the need; examination of alternative policies; ample elucidation of the preferred step toward free trade were treated with historical and other detail, and undergirded by a broad philosophy of this economic-political-international problem.

Ford's scanty speech training and general educational background gave little promise of his developing leadership as speaker, or of his catholic approach to these issues of management and labor, industrial production, and world-wide economic relationships. His freedom with an audience may be partly explained by his earlier qualities of sociability in preparatory school, in the United States Navy, at Yale, and as a worker in the Ford Dearborn plant before his ascendancy to the Ford presidency.

The student is advised to read the entire speech too long for complete inclusion here.

[1] Text furnished through the courtesy of Mr. Henry Ford II, with permission for this reprinting.

[2] For biographical note, see Appendix.

There is something I would like to talk about—and I believe that there is no more appropriate audience for my particular purpose than the newspaper editors and publishers of this great midwest area of the nation—the Inland Daily Press Association.

We are living in an age when faster and faster communication is being developed between greater and greater numbers of people. In our own lifetime, we have seen some fairly sensational developments. Airplanes have brought the towers of Chicago— including one or two of the ivory variety—within a few hours of London or Honolulu. The telephone has brought us even closer together, and the radio and television have made communication practically instantaneous.

Then, there is that other medium which some people say is even faster than instantaneous on occasion. I mean, of course, the press.

Certainly, therefore, this seems an appropriate time and place to discuss some of the problems that face us in communicating with other people. I say the place is important because, startling as it may seem to many Americans, our often-called "isolationist" Midwest is one of the great trading areas of the world. . . .

Fortunately the new Administration comes to power at a time when the climate of opinion both at home and abroad is ripe for an overhauling of our whole outlook on foreign economic policy. From both the old and new worlds we hear in mounting volume the cry: "Trade, Not Aid." These people want to buy *from* us. They want to sell *to* us. But they don't want to be *bought* and *sold* by us.

Most of us will pretty generally agree that economic aid was clearly necessary in the years immediately following the World War II.

First, we should write a new law without loopholes encouraging the most rapid possible elimination of all tariffs. By making gradual reductions in hardship cases, the few industries really seriously affected would have an opportunity to adapt themselves to new conditions. We should drop the Smoot-Hawley Tariff and the now outmoded Reciprocal Trade Agreements Act, which has been pretty well riddled with holes in its yearly treks through Congress.

Second, we should abandon completely the quota system, which is contrary to every principle of free enterprise. Under quotas, regardless of price, demand or any other factor, only a fixed amount of a product can come into the country.

I have heard of a serious proposal, with powerful backing, to place every single import under a quota based on present import levels. Such an act would not only immediately and permanently limit imports at present levels; it would gradually dry up all our trade as the pattern of demand rapidly shifted away from its present position. This, it seems to me, is the most dangerous kind of high-tariff thinking.

Third, we should abandon the Buy American Act. The effect of that Act is to prohibit the Federal and some state and local governments from buying foreign goods unless they are priced at least 25 per cent under the lowest domestic bid. Very few importers can make that low a bid, particularly after paying customs duties on their products.

The Federal Government alone now purchases about twenty billion dollars' worth of goods a year. Buy American may cost us as much as one half billion dollars a year, according to one estimate. If Buy American provisions and pressures were dropped, as well as import duties, an important stimulus to imports and large savings to the taxpayer would result.

Recently, for example, a foreign manufacturer, after paying a 45 per cent import duty, underbid two American firms by substantially more than 25 per cent on an Army contract. In subsequent bids, the Americans, oddly enough, were able to come down almost 50 per cent. That brought them just within the 25 per cent Buy American margin. The Army ultimately split the purchase between the American and foreign firms, saving you and me about half of the potential tax costs plus the import duties paid by the foreign firm—but appeasing at the same time the domestic producers.

Fourth, we should enact promptly a workable law for simplifying customs procedures. Many of those procedures have the intended purpose of submerging imports under a virtually impenetrable cascade of red tape. They tell me that down in Washington there are books of customs regulations just as thick as the Chicago phone book, of paper just as fine, and print just as small. . . .

Rightly or wrongly, the American people and most foreign peoples feel that American business will be a more powerful force in the councils of the new Administration. Rightly or wrongly, the Republican party and industry are associated in the minds of many peoples with high tariffs and isolationism. I think therefore, that a particularly great responsibility falls upon American industry to give the new Administration real suport in its efforts to strengthen the free world through "Trade, Not Aid." I think private enterprise must make a head-on assault on these problems, based on the managerial know-how and the spirit of venture which is the soul of our capitalist economy.

After all, what is needed more than American dollars and American goods in the world today is American business know-how. And by "know-how" I do not mean just the tricks and techniques of mass production. I mean our driving belief that no problem is insurmountable, and that nothing is being done as well as it could be done.

This is the one truly revolutionary force in the world today.

We have an unparalleled and long-awaited opportunity to bring that force into action. If we do so, then we can perhaps make this the beginning of a golden age in world history.

Will American industry recognize and accept this opportunity?

I hope we will.

A MARRIAGE OF BUSINESS AND EDUCATION [3]

ROBERT R. YOUNG [4]

Mr. Robert R. Young gave this address at the Barnard Forum, following a luncheon at the Waldorf-Astoria, on February 14, 1953. This Forum was sponsored by the alumnae of thirty-four women's colleges, who made the bulk of the audience.

Four speakers participated: President Wright, of Smith College; President Gallagher, of the City College of New York; Chancellor Heald, of New York University; and Mr. Young.

Each spoke for some fifteen minutes on the general topic, "A Decade of Decision for Higher Education." Following the addresses, each of the speakers discussed the problem with the others, and the panel was then questioned by the audience.

Mr. Young's speech although brief, is a survey of the broad problem of education. For him the problem is one of the need for education to face the situation of mounting leisure time; of the failure of the curriculum to attract sufficient numbers; of the need of education to help stem the movement toward standardization or collectivism; and of the need for creative thought to prevent the industrial "invasion of the field of learning and the bankruptcy of the higher institution of learning." His four concrete solutions are concluded by a proposal for action (a meeting at White Sulphur Springs to implement his ideas).

Young's style is epigrammatic, concrete, visual. He writes his own speeches and, we are informed, also a good deal of the copy that has distinguished the Chesapeake and Ohio public relations advertising. The present example is in the mood and method of such direct and attention-catching pronouncements.

Soft of voice, quiet, with spare figure, he is dynamic on his feet and impressive in his lively reaction to his ideas and in his ability to project to an audience.

Great stress has recently been placed upon the financial crisis faced by our higher institutions of learning, the nature and causes of which no one knows better than this audience.

A still greater crisis is faced by the cultural as opposed to the specialized education.

[3] Text supplied through the courtesy of Mr. Robert R. Young, with the privilege of this reprinting.

[4] For biographical note, see Appendix.

Out of these challenges of finance and of specialization can come a constructive revolution in education, one that is long overdue.

Having learned here in America to produce guns as well as butter, and now to fear a surplus of each, need we despair of the utility of education? The problems, rather, are:

(a) To preserve its independence,
(b) To broaden its scope,
(c) To channel constructively the vast revenue it produces,
(d) To direct wholesomely the leisure it affords.

If the educated man earns three times as much as the uneducated, can he consume three times as much and does it not behoove business to see that there are more of the educated? Certainly, business does not propose to plead guilty to the indictment that the only outlet for its productive genius is war.

Tomorrow we will produce with one coal miner the tonnage it took twenty miners to produce a generation ago. The newest plant of the Steel Corporation is described as a push button plant. These mounting powers to produce, this Frankenstein of production without labor, will force society to recognize with Thoreau that there is a place in life for culture as well as for work, and that education to that end can become as important to business as the most technical education.

When it does, Du Pont will find it possible to establish grants for the study of many things besides chemistry. Business, as supplier and taxpayer, has much at stake in healthy citizens, happy families and well-appointed homes. The sorry records of our public institutions, our relief rolls, our divorce and juvenile courts may not be the responsibility of our educators but they are none the less symptoms of deficiencies in our education.

If of women college graduates 35 per cent choose a career without marriage is it not because the curriculum has failed to attract those whose ambition is home making? And does not this startling fact concerning women suggest that there may be something equally wrong in what higher education offers to attract the boy? Perhaps a majority of the most talented of them, too, prefer to move along with life more quickly, both economically and domestically.

With less than half of our top 25 per cent in intelligence ever getting to college, and the common denominator of leisure a cocktail party, it is apparent that we have barely scratched the surface of higher education.

If this planet is to endure we must be taught that the path to truth is not a collective one, that it can be attained only through the independent and critical approach, that it is far more important to criticize than to commend, to dare than to conform. Men are not sheep nor mobs but fashion frequently decrees them to be so. The virtues of rugged individualism and private enterprise are surprisingly scarce even where they are most boasted. Nine business leaders out of ten will not express their own opinion on a delicate subject until they are sure of the popular view even though all nine of them know it is wrong, such is the power of opinion, even mistaken opinion. There is something inherently faulty in our teaching when this is so.

We cannot hope to solve today's complex problems without thought. But where and when are we taught the virtue of solitude without which constructive thought is scarcely possible? To be alone has almost become to be eccentric. My best work is done in an hour's walk along the ocean, but if the ordinary salaried business executive worked that way he would be fired. There are organizers of great businesses who have not yet been taught to organize their own lives. It is false notions of play, as well as crude habits of work, that make the typical wife of a successful executive a widow.

Unless education better helps us in meeting today's problems of living and better prepares us for the sharply competitive economic struggle that lies ahead, will not even fewer young men and women elect to devote four of their most formative and crucial years to the often lax and directionless routine of the campus, eyes turned back to so much that is old when there is so much new threatening to run them down. His television set, the comics, drive home to every youngster the fact that many of his text books are out of date before the type is set.

Thirty years ago one of my superiors advised me not to bother to read current articles dealing with business. He said, "Those who have anything worth while to say are too busy to write it." He may have been wrong but it is true that unless institutional education keeps pace vocational and professional training can become a function of the hospitals, the work shops, the counting houses and laboratories of industry. The unmatched handiwork of the past came out of the guilds with their apprentice system, not out of the schools. What has been true of the skills can become true of all industry. Once such a trend starts the invasion of the field of education by business can bankrupt our higher institutions of learning, or, reduce them to a mere appendage of the Federal Government.

If our beginners in higher education were offered the privilege of alternating between college and business, hospital or law office, in equal relays of three, four or six months, business to pay the costs, would not business and education both benefit? Would not our colleges have more beginners and our businesses better suited ones? How much more intelligent would be the choice they finally make of a career? Under such a system our institutions of learning, like our businesses, would function continuously throughout the seasons; no more would future doctors or engineers spend their summers washing dishes.

And this leads me to another proposal. Our higher institutions of learning should embark upon an aggressive promotion of education among adults. If we have gone from the sixty-hour week to the forty-hour week within our memories, can we not soon go to a thirty- or even a twenty-five-hour week, and will time not hang even heavier on our hands? Education has given inadequate recognition to this revolutionary change that has so recently come into our lives. Unaccustomed to our idle hours, is it surprising that they are often ill spent?

If truth and beauty and integrity are forgotten and the fields of culture become fallow, the advancing years barer, not richer, is it not because we have neglected to cultivate in the best season?

It has been well said that education as well as youth can be wasted on the young. Is it not more logical for the organized pursuit of culture to accompany or follow economic success than it is for it to precede it? Cadillac does not direct its sales energies to the young and unemployed but to those who have attained a competence. The awakening of an appreciation for the finer things in life can be more important after forty than under twenty. How many in this room, if they were adequately pensioned, or had attained some degree of financial independence, would like to study music, gardening, painting, or even Greek? Our pension funds and insurance tables tell us America is becoming filled with such people, and our psychiatrists tell us that no one so needs wholesome occupation as the retired and often lonely man or woman. The yearning for knowledge, culture and companionship such as education can give continues until the eyes are finally closed.

On the vocational side in the middle age groups I have many railroad executives badly in need of specialized instruction in certain phases of their work for which the railroad would pay a competent institution of learning handsomely. We, in the railroad business, need a clearinghouse for the interchange of the most advanced ideas and methods used on all our 130 great railroads in all departments. There are problems of ticketing, refrigeration, bearings, brakes, commutation, express, equipment, terminals. I can think of scores where the promise of reward to our stockholders from such an up-to-the-minute education center would be, to steal the title of a recently published book, Merely Colossal. I am sure other industries suffer as costly deficiencies in the specialized education of their upper age groups. If education does not offer such clearinghouses for every industry business sooner or later will.

To escape this imminent danger of the perversion of education to pure utility, the engulfment of education by business, as dangerous to freedom as its subsidy by the Federal Government, there must be a marriage of business and education, each a vital partner, neither subordinate to the other. Only thus can the needs of business be met, cultural values sustained, and individual liberty preserved.

And just as the cross-fertilization of students and workers in the system I envisage would cause business and education both to flourish, so would more elbow-rubbing and an actual interchange of teachers and executives help to wipe out today's mutual distrust. Students would gain in more experienced and practical professors, employees in more understanding and better-rounded bosses. Natural inclinations and abilities would find faster and fuller expression. Teacher pay, never adequate, and losing further ground with each new round of wage increases, would move to full parity, for it would be too apparent that the qualities required of the good teacher are no less rare than those of the good executive. Being equal sharers in the same system, teacher, student, employer and employee, all would become equal proponents of it. Business and education, instead of becoming servants of the State, would continue its masters.

Today there are only two million enrolled in our higher institutions of learning. There should be eight million. Present enrollment of the young can easily be doubled, simply by making higher education more immediately useful and self-sustaining. It can be doubled again by aggressively selling all ages, those most able to afford and competent to receive education. Our educational institutions can then be no less self-sustaining and prosperous than our businesses.

To recapitulate, I would:

(1) Broaden the cultural scope of education by teaching many things essential to good citizenship now virtually untouched such as healthful, wholesome living, good home-making and good parenthood, discipline and self-discipline.

(2) So organize that one half of the time of the youth undergoing higher education is shared with business so that it may be more effective and self-supporting, hence more universal.

(3) Make of our universities and colleges industry clearinghouses for the advanced technical education of executives.

(4) Aggressively sell higher education, cultural and specialized, to all ages.

(5) Establish equality of pay and a system of interchange of teachers and executives to the end of more proficient professors and better bosses.

I have asked Mr. Tuohy, President of the Chesapeake and Ohio Railway to invite certain heads of colleges and of businesses in its trade area to join in finding ways and means of putting these proposals, which are not new or original, into operation. Our meeting with these guests from education and business will be in June, the month of marriages; the place, White Sulphur Springs, West Virginia, at our Greenbrier Hotel, rendezvous of honeymooners since 1778.

This is not an academic discussion. It is a concrete proposal to more firmly root our unmatched American system of incentive enterprise, call it democracy or republic.

To make sure that at least the second of these proposals escapes becoming academic, to insure the consummation of the marriage, the various companies with which I am associated, including many diverse industries besides railroads, here and now offer to find places for many student-worker relays. These students will divide their time between job and study, their work assignments directly related to their future ambitions. Some may thus find their niche and conclude their education in one or two years, some not for five or even ten years. What matters the length of the first dip into higher education if it is to be only the first?

TIDELANDS OIL [5]

SPESSARD L. HOLLAND [6]

Senator Spessard L. Holland, of Florida, opened the Senate debate on Senate Joint Resolution 13, providing for giving to the states "property rights in the submerged lands beneath navigable waters." The bill had already passed the House. In effect the bill was to fulfill the Republican position in the presidential campaign, to give Florida, Louisiana, Texas, and California, rights to the tidelands oil claimed by these respective states.

Senator Holland's lengthy debate opened the prolonged Senate discussion of this problem. For an illustration of the opposing point of view, see Senator Lehman's speech below.

Senator Holland had been a member of the debating team at Emory College, editor of the college magazine, and from his college days, had established a reputation as effective debater and public speaker. His extended career as lawyer and office holder had also much strengthened his platform ability.

Mr. President, the subject of Senate Joint Resolution 13 is property, property rights in the submerged lands beneath navigable waters. By way of a brief summary, the general purpose of this measure as reported by the Interior and Insular Affairs Committee is to recognize, confirm, establish, and vest in and assign to the respective states the title and ownership of the lands and resources beneath navigable waters within their respective boundaries, as well as the right and power to manage, administer, lease, develop, and use these lands and resources in accordance with applicable state law. The transfer of property rights in the submerged lands and resources to the several states from the Federal Government is made subject to the exercise by the Federal Government of all its powers of regulation for the purpose of commerce, navigation, national defense, and international affairs, all of which powers shall continue to be paramount to, but shall not be deemed to include, proprietary rights of ownership and development. Of course, such lands as the

---

[5] *Congressional Record.* 99:2848 and 2877, April 6, 1953 (daily edition).
[6] For biographical note, see Appendix.

United States itself has acquired in a proprietary capacity by eminent domain procedure, purchase, cession, gift, or otherwise shall remain the property of the Federal Government.

This joint resolution also revokes as to all areas within the boundaries of the states the misconceived and ill-advised action of former President Truman, in his attempt to make a naval petroleum reserve of all the submerged lands within the entire continental shelf. It is unfortunate that Mr. Truman added confusion to this complicated and controversial issue by such action when, as shown by the official departmental memoranda of the Department of Justice, he had been advised that he was not creating a naval reserve within the meaning of the statute on that subject. Attorney General Brownell, when questioned on this matter in the hearings before Subcommittee Number 1 of the Committee on the Judiciary, House of Representatives, on February 17, 1953, stated that the executive order signed by Mr. Truman on January 16, 1953—and I now quote Mr. Brownell—"merely transferred the administrative power over these lands from one department to another, and did not set up a naval petroleum reserve within the meaning of the statute." Attorney General Brownell further stated in a letter dated February 13, 1953, addressed to the Secretary of ·Defense, that "it was also clear that the then Attorney General, Judge McGranery, approved the order, as finally drafted and issued, on the understanding that it did not intend to nor did it in fact or in law create a naval petroleum reserve within the meaning of the statute."

It will be noted that this joint resolution provides that nothing therein shall be deemed to affect in any wise the rights of the United States to the natural resources of the portion of the subsoil and seabed of the continental shelf lying outside the boundaries of the respective states, and it confirms the jurisdiction and control of the Federal Government over those natural resources. In other words, this measure clearly emphasizes that nine tenths of the submerged lands off the coast of the United States is under the control and jurisdiction of the Federal Government and that the other one tenth, which lies inside the boundaries of the states, and immediately adjoining the coasts of the states, should be owned and controlled by the respective states. . . .

In closing, it is interesting to note that many of those who oppose this proposed legislation are the very ones who have been active proponents of an ever larger Federal Government and who seem to think that an all-powerful Federal Government is a panacea for all the ills of the people of this country. Those of us who support the proposed legislation are strongly opposed to the nationalization of resources—and that is what they are attempting to do to us—in the five-thousand-mile shoestring of coastal waters which throttles the shores of our coastal states. The resources in this narrow belt are vital to the states and to local growth and prosperity, and we feel that the ownership and control of these resources should remain in the states and be subjected to state and local control where it will be very close to the people who are so greatly affected.

We are now talking about fundamental philosophy. We are talking about local self-government. We are talking about the opportunity of a citizen to see the very officials who serve him in the regulation of lands which may represent the total investment of his lifetime savings. We think it is sound government to keep such regulation, control, and ownership just as close to home as is possible.

We strongly feel that our position is sound and just, that it will receive, as it has already received, the approval of the vast majority of our people who, we believe, as indicated by the result of the recent Gallup poll, agree with us that the important rights enjoyed by the states for a hundred and fifty years should be restored and safeguarded, and that such action would be in the interest of soundly economic and democratic government. These rights and the immense values already developed and to be developed in the coastal belt, plus the similar values in the inland waters and in the Great Lakes, involve problems which are so clearly local in nature that we shall continue with all of our strength to fight to prevent their transfer to a Federal Government which is already too big, too wasteful, and too far from the people.

Mr. President, there is not a senator within the sound of my voice who does not know that much of the body of ills which afflict us on the domestic front flows directly from the fact that the Federal Government is too big, and that there is no finite mind which can grasp all its implications or all its details, even though it is the responsibility of senators and representatives to make laws for the government of our huge, swollen Federal system, as well as of our people, and it is our duty to provide appropriations whereby those immense pieces of uncoordinated machinery can attempt to function.

It is our hope that the joint resolution will speedily pass the Senate and be enacted into law.

TIDELANDS OIL [7]

HERBERT H. LEHMAN [8]

Senator Herbert H. Lehman, of New York, gave an extended debate on the tidelands oil issue, on April, 13, 1953, in answer to Senator Holland and other proponents of the resolution. Only the introduction, to set forth the issues from his point of view, is here included.

For a full examination of this Senate debate, preceding its final adoption, the student is advised to read the *Congressional Record* for the month of April 1953. Some of the most vigorous debates of recent Senate history are there presented.[9]

Mr. President, the question before us is simple.

It is not, primarily, a legal problem.

It is not a question of who is right. It is more of a question of what is right. In a major sense the pending question is a moral question.

I am not a lawyer, as my colleagues know.

It is not necessary to be a lawyer to vote on this bill. Perhaps it is even a handicap.

The legal cases cited in this debate are interesting. But most of them are beside the main point.

The main point is this: Why should we vote to give away these vital and valuable offshore oil resources—these resources in the land beds beneath the sea?

Why should we vote to abdicate the national government's power to regulate what goes on in the open sea and in the land beds beneath the sea?

Why should we vote to give Texas, Louisiana, and California the exclusive key to a national treasure said to be worth fifty billion dollars—perhaps much more than that?

The Supreme Court has ruled that this treasure, these rights, and this regulatory power are vested in the Federal Government.

---

[7] *Congressional Record.* 99:3077. April 13, 1953 (daily edition).

[8] For biographical note, see Appendix.

[9] For further comment on Senator Lehman, see Herbert Lehman, "This I Believe," *Representative American Speeches: 1951-1952*, p90.

The Supreme Court made that decision in three separate cases.

That is the law.

Why should we vote to overrule the Supreme Court?

Most of the arguments made in this debate have been over the question of whether the Supreme Court was right.

We have been retrying the case.

That is an interesting exercise. I have received much profit from this phase of the debate. But that is not our function or our jurisdiction.

We must not lose sight of the main question before us, much as the proponents of this legislation would like to have us lose sight of that question.

That question is: Why should we give these rights away? Why should we give these billions away?

Under the rulings of the Supreme Court these rights and this great wealth belong to all the states—to New York, and Connecticut, and Virginia, and Ohio, and Wisconsin, and Minnesota, and North Dakota, and Iowa—to all the forty-eight states and all the people of this country and to their descendants.

Why should Congress vote to take these rights away from all the people, from the nation as a whole, and give them to three states?

The proponents of this legislation have not given the answer. In my remarks today, Mr. President, I shall try to state why the Congress should not give these rights away. I propose to argue what I deeply believe, that the national interest and the national need require the retention of these rights, and that the alienation of these rights—this proposed giveaway—is a denial of the national interest, and a handicap to our national security.

What we should be doing, Mr. President, in the proper exercise of our obligations as members of the national Congress, is to be debating how best to use these rights to promote the national interest and to advance the national security—not what manner we can legally follow in giving away these rights which lawfully belong to the nation.

The Anderson bill offers a method of using the rights lawfully vested in the national government—to develop our oil resources, to expand our oil production, to promote the national defense, and incidentally to award to the states adjacent to these resources a very generous share of the benefits from the development of these resources, within the three-mile area.

The Hill amendment offers a way of using the benefits accruing to the national government to promote the general welfare of the nation by advancing the cause of education throughout our land, by investing part of the Federal Government's share of the proceeds from this development in the future of America, in the education of our young. In my opinion, nothing could possibly be more important.

The Holland joint resolution neglects these needs entirely. It concentrates on a confused and questionable formula for giving away what can be given away, and for paralyzing the national government's access to those rights which cannot, even under the most extreme stretch of the legal imagination, be given away.

The national rights of the three-mile belt are proposed to be given away. The bill proposes to give away title, but comprehends the strong possibility that title cannot be given away, and so provides for the contingency that this part of the giveaway will be declared illegal. So the Holland joint resolution proposes to give away the rights to the resources in the three-mile belt, even if the courts find that Congress could not legally hand over the legal title to this area.

Then the Holland measure goes further, and edges out beyond the three-mile zone, into the international zone, and seeks to give to certain states title to areas in the open sea beyond any limits which our country has ever claimed to be the exclusive territory of any country, even our own.

We have protested and resisted the claims of Russia, Ecuador, and Mexico, among other nations, to exclusive territorial rights beyond the three-mile zone off their shores; but today it is proposed to give to certain states proprietary rights to ocean areas far beyond our coasts—rights which we as a nation have never claimed to possess.

What a travesty on national responsibility. How irresponsible we will seem in the eyes of the world if we approve this legislation.

Of course, Mr. President, we have claimed, and will continue to claim, certain regulatory powers over the continental shelf, as far out as it may extend. But this claim must be maintained in the international sphere, by the United States as a nation; and any rights which accrue to this nation as a result of our successful contention in this sphere belong to the nation as a whole, and should not and cannot be given away to certain states, to the prejudice of the whole nation. . . .

INTELLECTUAL IDEALS

HISTORICAL PERSPECTIVE
AND CURRENT ISSUES [1]

GRAYSON KIRK [2]

Dr. Grayson Kirk, then vice president and provost, and since January 1953, president of Columbia University, gave this commencement address at the University on June 5, 1952.

The speaker's approach was by way of his special field of government and his recent experiences on the spot with European leaders and their problems. His thesis—the need for perspective—was especially timely. Much American reaction, especially of World War II and Korean veterans and their households, was pessimistic, even cynical.

The argument here for a well-balanced view of events to be surveyed through broad perspective was developed by a candid analysis of the domestic and international scene as of June 1952. It was a pretty dismal outlook.

The speaker's bases for optimism—the progress of the Schuman plan, of the NATO, and of the United Nations, of the absence of World War III—were well taken. Cynics from the vantage point of 1953 may weigh in detail each of his propositions. How sound were President Kirk's assumptions and conclusions? Had not the United Nations of 1953 deteriorated? Was the passing of Stalin not the milestone in stepped up hostilities? Had official morality under Eisenhower markedly improved? Were congressional investigations by Senator McCarthy and others more damaging on the whole than otherwise?

The address was well organized. The personal quality was obvious (with some twenty-four "I's" and additional pronouns). The ideas were often cautious generalizations. What some of his audience wanted the speaker to say was, "Eisenhower has just landed to begin his primary campaign. I hope he will beat out Taft at Chicago next month and will win in November against Trumanism. Therefore support Eisenhower." Obviously a university president could hardly so talk. President Kirk's address, nevertheless, was basically well reasoned, timely, and well up to the standards of scores of similar addresses given by Nicholas Murray Butler.

[1] Text and permission for this reprint supplied through the courtesy of President Kirk.

[2] For biographical note, see Appendix.

This is the season when, all over our country, thousands of young men and women are compelled to listen to one final address before they can assume the new dignities of the degree for which their years of study have qualified them. My own experience has been that commencement speeches generally can be divided into two classes. One is an address which could have been given almost as well at any other public function; it bears little or no relationship to the actual ceremony. The other is of a familiar pattern. The young graduates are warned in the most solemn fashion that the world is in a truly desperate condition. Vast dangers threaten the individual and society on every hand. These perils can be conquered only if the young people—who are the hope of the world—will shoulder their responsibilities, will utilize to the fullest the knowledge they have gained in college, and will proceed to lead civilization out of the morass and up on to the sunlit plains of security and progress.

The net effect of such speeches would be to dispel all the fine gaiety and pleasure of a commencement day and send the graduates creeping away, filled to the brim with gloomy forebodings about the life which awaits them. I say, "would be," advisedly because, happily, a commencement speech, of all forms of public addresses, undoubtedly is given least attention by its hearers. Not even the most direful prophet of doom really can dissipate the happiness of a day properly to be enjoyed by those who have worked long and hard to receive the recognition which the ceremony brings to them.

And so, today, in what I regard as the proper spirit of Commencement, I would like to be unorthodox to some degree at least and to urge upon you—the newest members of our proud roster of degree-holders—the need, not for grim pessimism, but for perspective. And I say flatly, and without those qualifications dear to the academic mind, that, on balance, the present is more of a time for optimism than for bleak despair. It is a time when I would say to you, *"Sursum Corda"* and not *"Carpe Diem."*

In saying this, I am properly aware of the momentous problems of our time. Their gravity is amply illustrated by the fact that our president has had to be on leave for the past eighteen months to organize the defense of the free world. I am mindful of the menacing power which lies behind the Soviet conspiracy against the non-Communist world. I am well aware of the gains which have been made by the plotters in the Kremlin—and of those which they still may be able to make. I also realize the political and economic weaknesses of our chief allies, the absence of inspiring leadership within our democratic societies, and the burden of national debt and economic instability which plagues us at home. I am also not unmindful of the scandalously low levels of morality demonstrated by so many persons in whom public trust has been misplaced.

Why, then, do I urge upon you a feeling of cautious optimism and the need for perspective in making your judgments? I do so, first of all, because our democratic heritage and the welfare of our society demand that our people estimate both sides of the picture before they rush to value judgments or to policy conclusions. And I have had the feeling of late that many of our fellow-citizens have become so obsessed with our troubles, so conscious of our perils, so afflicted with nostalgia for a vanished past, that they tend to underestimate such progress as we are making and, even more, the prospects for the future. We can err by too much pessimism almost as badly as by too much optimism. Cassandra does not necessarily offer us better counsel than Pollyanna.

To be sure, the Soviet menace is deadly, but let us remember that, in the face of it, the democracies have joined forces to a degree unprecedented in peace-time history. Not only is a vast program of rearmament under way, but it is a program based on the principles of unified resistance to a common danger. Who among us here today would have believed a few years ago that any menace, however great, could have produced in Western Europe a Schuman plan and an agreement on a European army drawn from the member nations that have so recently and so bloodily fought among themselves? Who would have believed that the United States would have taken part—and even a major role—in creating the North Atlantic community of nations? Who would have believed that despite the strife which rends the world, we could continue to have international organization in which all the great powers would retain their membership? No one of these events is in itself a development capable of assuring peace and security for our time, but, taken together, they do represent a degree of progress which, in the long perspective of history, is both remarkable and encouraging.

Let us also remember that our enemies, at the time of our greatest weakness and disunity, have not unleashed upon the world the horrors of a general war, but have contented themselves with their familiar tools of propaganda, subversion, infiltration and limited wars, as in Korea, which, though costly, have had a catalytic effect upon the latent forces of military strength and political unity in the West. I say to you frankly that I would not like to be in the shoes of those Soviet officials whose schemes have succeeded so well that they have unified against the USSR the most powerful assemblage of potential force in the history of the world.

While no one can look into the seeds of time and tell which will grow and which will not, I do believe that, if we are firm, far-sighted in our planning, and we make an effort to understand the conditions of peace as well as war, we may be able to work through this agonizing period of tension to some acceptable form of coexistence. Our enemies may force conflict upon us, but if this does not happen, we must understand that excessive rigidity in our own thinking can be dangerous to our own best interests. I make no plea for appeasement toward the Kremlin and its conspiracy, but I do plead for sober thought on our part concerning the conditions of coexistence which we are prepared to accept. We must be prepared both for war and for peace. And let us not fall into the dangerous conclusion that there is such a thing as inevitable war.

Time, I think, is on our side. Otherwise, we will have been wrong in all our thinking about the strength of the ideals of human freedom and democracy. But time alone is not enough, and we cannot assume that we can sit idly by while it works for us. Time will continue to be on our side only if we have the wisdom to utilize to the fullest the opportunities which it may bring. Time alone will not bring us into an apocalyptic era when all men are brothers and when peace will reign supreme forever-more, but if we use our immense strength skillfully, patiently, and with foresight, time gradually may forge those bonds of collaboration among nations which will give us the prospect that our disputes will be settled without resort to force. The worst service that we can do for ourselves and for the world is to conclude that we have no hope for anything but future war. Such a conclusion is mere fatalism; it is not rational judgment.

When we think of our own assets at home we refer customarily to our giant industrial strength, the advanced state of our science and technology as evidenced by our great advances in the utilization of nuclear energy, our vast manpower, and our unrivaled financial position. All these are fundamental, but there is something else which is even more important as a justification for a calm optimism about our future. This is our continued political unity. The violence of our party strife sometimes causes foreign observers to underestimate the degree of this unity. We must be careful that we do not allow ourselves to be deceived by it as well. The important thing is that, while we may differ profoundly over issues of policy, and while we may feel that our political opponents are reckless, ill-advised and hopelessly incompetent, we do not contemplate destroying our constitutional system to make our particular views prevail. I am convinced that the greatest force for peace in the world today is the unshakable political unity of the American people.

It is of the highest importance that we make the outside world understand that our domestic policy quarrels, deriving largely from differences over the proper role of government in an increasingly industrialized society, do not—and will not—affect to the slightest degree our common loyalty to the basic principles and procedures of our constitutional system.

When we tend to be downhearted about our situation, I wonder how we would feel if we Americans were in the situation of our French allies, where the Communists have had recently as high as 30 per cent of the popular votes. And I wonder how gloomy we should be if we were geographically in the situation of the Norwegians or the Turks with respect to Soviet power.

And I wonder how we would feel if our economic situation were as unpromising as that of Britain.

Perspective is also important in evaluating the level of morality on the part of our public officials. Though no responsible citizen can condone the activities of persons who have shown themselves unworthy of the public trust which has been confided in them, let us remember that no society has ever been wholly free from this blight. There will always be little men who will use power for selfish ends, but let us be thankful that we have a society in which, through the vigilance of a free press, these men can be exposed. And let us also be thankful that we have a political and a judicial system which will enable us to punish these men and to replace them. Consider for a moment what our plight would be if we were living in a nondemocratic society where we had no free press to bring criminality to light and no political means, through free elections, to bring about an orderly change.

You may ask, "Why, on this commencement day, do you take pains to remind us of these national assets? And why do you so stress the need for a balanced judgment and the use of a full historical perspective in weighing the issues of our times?" My answer is that I do so because you are now members of a vast fellowship of nearly two hundred thousand men and women, in all countries and in all walks of life, who have achieved the distinction of Columbia degrees. This university is one of the greatest cultural assets of our country. It is a truly national university whose influence radiates to the corners of the world. For the remainder of your lives you are an integral part of Columbia, and if you manifest these qualities of perspective and calm judgment, your influence will have public importance and you will justify our faith in you and our service to the society which has created and maintained this university. By your works we shall be judged.

For nearly two centuries, Columbia graduates have served this nation. They have preached from its pulpits, written its books, edited its newspapers, made its laws, administered its government, and they have died bravely on its battlefields. We have given to the United States thousands of leaders of wisdom, integrity and unfailing courage. Today, when so many of our fellow-citizens seem to view the future "as through a glass darkly," it is up to you to demonstrate that you have faith in America, that you have an abiding devotion to the principles of human freedom, and that you have full confidence that this country, under God, will do all in its power to help lead the world toward a new era of civilization and peace.

THE FOES OF THE HUMANITIES [3]

Monroe E. Deutsch [4]

Dr. Monroe Deutsch, vice president and provost emeritus of the University of California, gave this address at a dinner session of the Western College Association, held at the Biltmore Hotel, Los Angeles, California, on January 6, 1953.

The speaker has had a long and distinguished career as teacher, administrator, and public speaker. His theme of the humanities was in the vein of his long defense of liberal college training. In this speech, his background and appreciation of history and literature strongly enriched his premises. The concluding passages of the speech were original and deeply eloquent. Reported Charles T. Fitts, Secretary of the Association, "At the conclusion of the stirring address, the speaker, a much admired past president of the Association, was given an ovation." [5]

To be perfectly frank, I am not wholly clear as to a definition of the humanities or what fields of study are included under that term. Webster defines it: "The branches of polite learning regarded as primarily conducive to culture; especially, the ancient classics and belles-lettres; sometimes secular, as distinguished from theological learning." This definition does not seem very helpful. I really don't know what branches of learning are "polite" nor "regarded as primarily conducive to culture."

Perhaps the words of Terence may be sufficiently broad to take in everything that should be covered: "*Homo sum: humani nihil a me alienum puto.* (I am a man: I think naught that is human [humanum] alien to me.") In short, what is concerned with human beings may be regarded as falling under the humanities in the broadest sense of the term. Excluded are the subjects that deal with matter as opposed to man. Physics and chemistry and engineering are examples of fields outside of the humanities.

Accordingly the social sciences may be classed in the humanities. Certainly, history deals with man and his achievements. But

[3] Text furnished through the courtesy of Dr. Deutsch, with permission for this reprint.

[4] For biographical note, see Appendix.

[5] For further comment on Dr. Deutsch, see *Representative American Speeches: 1942-1943*, p218.

political science, concerned with mankind in its ways of governing itself, is also to be included. And so too is economics which deals with the manner by which mankind makes and earns a living.

And yet I wonder whether the latter fields are not concerned especially with mankind externally rather than with the spirit of man.

In the humanities I should certainly count music and art. For they are the work of humans and have no meaning save in their effect on humans. And while the noblest examples of each assuredly deserve to be placed beside the masterpieces of literature, we shall agree, I think, that works of letters can reach more of mankind and their messages are clearer; besides each of us can choose those that have meaning for him, and we do not need the external aid of works of art in galleries or music performed by musicians.

The core of the humanities is in my judgment literature—whether in our own tongue or a foreign one. It is literature which teaches us how to live. Nor should I hesitate to include philosophy and history too; you recall that Clio is one of the muses.

Think of all that these fields cover—the works of philosophy and of fiction, the tragedies and the comedies, the orations, the epics, the lyrics, the histories. What a glorious phalanx they form and how they raise us above the mundane and make us see life as something infinitely greater than the tasks which furnish us our daily bread!

They teach us not what the physical world about us is but what we ourselves are and what we may be. They are the best teachers, the best guides, in the life we live during these few decades of ours.

They not only raise us to higher spiritual levels but help us in our relations with our fellows and in the pursuit of our own lives. They are for living far more important than a knowledge of the physical sciences, far more important than information concerning the machinery of government or the laws of economics. Do not mistake me; for a well-rounded life these things too are necessary. We live in a physical universe, we are citizens of a state, and food and shelter depend upon economic conditions.

Walter Lippmann said some twelve years ago in an address wisely delivered before the American Association for the Advancement of Science:

> Modern education, however, is based on a denial that it is necessary, or useful, or desirable for the schools and colleges to continue to transmit from generation to generation the religious and classical culture of the Western world. . . . It abandons and neglects as no longer necessary the study of the whole classical heritage of the great works of great men. . . . The emancipated democracies have renounced the idea that the purpose of education is to transmit the Western culture. Thus, there is a cultural vacuum, and the cultural vacuum was bound to produce, in fact it has produced, progressive disorder. For the more men have become separated from the spiritual heritage which binds them together, the more has education become egoist, careerist, specialist and asocial.

And these teachers of ours are of all nationalities, of all periods, of all languages. They include Plato and Thucydides, Virgil and Horace, Goethe and Schiller, Molière and Montaigne, Dante and Cervantes, Shakespeare and Milton, Emerson and Whitman. They make us realize the oneness of humanity and how alike in essentials life is, whether or not we possess automobiles, radio, telephones and television. One of the great merits of the humanities is that they show the real unity of mankind. When we deal with the thoughts of great writers, whatever the language in which they are written, we feel nothing alien in them; what they say is all that matters, and there is nothing foreign there save the language in which it is expressed. I know no better method of creating international understanding —yes, and admiration—than through a thoughtful study of the writings of the great figures of all lands.

What then has happened to the humanities in our time and our land? Why is it that letters are pushed aside? First and foremost responsible is the attitude of society to the whole business of education. It is assumed nowadays that young people go to college primarily to learn a profession, to fit themselves to become lawyers, physicians, dentists, architects, engineers, and the like. In short, the implied question always is: "Does this course help me to become an architect?" These professional curricula now have an underpinning of preprofessional courses. Yet the years preceding entry into law school or medical school were assumed to be periods for the education of human beings, not merely lawyers or physicians. The preprofessional courses and the emphasis on measuring all courses in the curriculum from the standpoint of their utility in the particular profession—these are enemy number one, the first foe of the humanities.

But it is not only the strictly professional curricula that are enemies of the humanities. The entire system which over-emphasizes a major subject in the junior and senior years, and sets aside so much of the two preceding years to preparation for the major, is equally dangerous. A prospective geologist is as shackled in his program as a prospective physician. Here, too, courses are weighed on the basis of their utility to the geologist. The effort is made to turn out a specialist at the time the bachelor's degree is conferred instead of looking forward to graduate study as the proper period for a high degree of specialization.

Of course, behind these two foes stands society which has all too often forgotten why universities and colleges exist, what they were intended to be, and thinks of them only as furnishing tools whereby a living may be earned.

In the recent work *They Went to College*, divers opinions as to the value of college and the value of different types of programs are expressed. One letter reads: "It is regrettable that culture is inedible." The term indeed that these graduates use is "culture," and there is in many cases behind it a sneer, as in this letter:

> Culture courses are no longer needed to occupy a parlor or drawing room chair. Conversations over the tables of night clubs, beer gardens, baseball games, and trolley car seats do not smack of French, Gothic architecture, or why the Greek oratory was superior to our own.[7]

In discussing such a point of view, Professor Fred B. Millett in his work *The Rebirth of Liberal Education* says:

> The normal extraverted American characteristically finds his values in things, not in ideas or attitudes, or in the possession of immaterial

goods. Despite his good nature and his generosity, despite his ready response to human suffering, he finds the most defensible human goal in the successful life, rather than the good life, and for him the most incontestable measure of success is the possession of things.

Years ago Bliss Perry delivered an address at the University of California on poetry. After its conclusion President Benjamin Ide Wheeler assembled a little group in the library of his home. Among others present was D. O. Mills, banker and regent. On meeting Professor Perry he "pronounced with finality: 'Mr. Perry, Poetry is a fine thing, but Business is *the* thing.'"

Another foe of the humanities is assuredly the lack of reading—especially of books by our people. Newspapers—at least the headlines—are commonly read, though it must be admitted that the comics and the sport pages are the sections of the papers most quickly perused. Magazines—save perhaps for those abundantly supplied with pictures or dealing with movie stars—fall behind newspapers in popularity. And books recede still further. And in this case it is fiction—I should say current fiction—that far exceeds the reading of nonfiction. Even fiction of a few years ago is far less often taken out of libraries. Everyone wants to be up-to-date, even if that means reading trash. Advertising beats the drum for it, and I sometimes suspect that occasionally book reviewers are strongly influenced by the advertising pages. Plato and Goethe and Milton—and even Emerson—do not compete for popular favor with *Forever Amber* and similar so-called pieces of literature.

Yet another of the foes of the humanities is the belief that a requirement in English in school or college is intended merely or at least primarily for the purpose of teaching the student to write acceptable English, to learn how to paragraph, how to spell, how to avoid the obvious errors in writing. How often the reading and study of literature is either neglected or at least pushed into a subordinate position! Do not misunderstand me— we should of course learn how to write good English. I wonder whether absorption in great literature is not itself one of the best teachers.

Are there, however, not other foes aside from the external ones of which I have spoken?

First of all, since our departments are always departments of language and literature, we tend to busy ourselves (I dare to say) too much with language, too little with literature. For example, instead of discussing the ideas with which the masters of letters deal, we tend to deal with translation. And if a student, by use of a dictionary gives the equivalent of the words the author has used, he wins an "A" and the class moves on to the next sentence. When you think of the pains which the author took to choose precisely the right words with the right shading, the student's translation is to his wording as a child's drawing is to that of a master artist.

A book is a repository of ideas, not merely a collection of words, to be discussed as words. If the latter were the case, would we be doing anything much more valuable than arranging beads by their color or their size? A great work is the result of the agony of a great mind; there are as truly labor pains as when a child enters the world. Think of Virgil and the time he took to write a page, to choose the right word, the one that most accurately depicted the idea struggling for expression. And how casually the word is chosen in an alien tongue to translate what he took such pains to select!

We must go beyond the words he uses to the ideas. In short, it is our duty to deal with literature as the expression of ideas, not as an assemblage of foreign words. When I say this, I say nothing at all new. Thus, John Milton in treating of education said:

> Seeing every nation affords not experience and tradition enough for all kinds of learning, therefore we are chiefly taught the languages of those people who have at any time been most industrious after wisdom; so that language is but the instrument conveying to us things useful to be known. And though a linguist should pride himself to have all the tongues that Babel cleft the world into; yet if he have not studied the solid things in them, as well as the words and lexicons, he were nothing so much to be esteemed a learned man as any yeoman or tradesman competently wise in his mother dialect only.

Another foe is the notion that information is all important, is the mark of an intelligent man or woman. Have you observed this in radio programs? The one entitled "Information Please" is a perfect illustration. Listeners attend enthusiastically when some prominent figure in public life or the stage, shows himself able to answer a host of factual questions. And yet one may not be able to tell what flowers are mentioned in Shakespeare and still understand Shakespeare fully. Professor R. M. MacIver of Columbia University has a pertinent example: "I have a recollection of being at a doctoral examination, a Ph.D. examination, where questions like this were hurled at the candidate who was thereby qualifying to be called a doctor of philosophy: 'Who was the postmaster general at the time of President Coolidge?'"

And Woodrow Wilson "often related with relish the answer he once found on an examination paper: 'This question is unfair. It requires thought.'"

Woodrow Wilson (to quote him once more) said wisely:

There is no discipline in information. Some of the best informed men I ever met could not reason at all. You know what you mean by an extraordinarily well-informed man. You mean a man who always has some fact at his command to trip you up; and you will generally find that all this man can do is to throw little chunks of fact in the way so that you will stumble on them and make yourself ridiculous. And if you say, "Very well, please be kind enough to generalize on this matter," you will find he cannot do it. Information is not education. Information is the raw material of education, but it is not education.

Abraham Flexner in *Universities: American, English, German* says:

The world has not lost, and, unless it is to lose its savor, will never lose the pure, appreciative, humanistic spirit—the love of beauty, the concern for ends established by ideals that dare to command rather than to obey. Now science, while widening our vision, increasing our satisfactions, and solving our problems, brings with it dangers peculiarly its own. We can become so infatuated with progress—in knowledge and control—both of which I have unstintedly emphasized—that we lose our perspective, lose our historic sense, lose a philosophic outlook, lose sight of relative cultural values.

Now I enter territory filled with ground-mines, extremely dangerous. Are not our teachers—I refer to teachers of the humanities—all too often trained in what one would call a "scientific" manner? And do they not feel that it is their function to deal with their subject matter "scientifically," i.e., factually? Are not our teachers dragooned from first to last to look at works of letters as quarries into which to dig, rather than as the expressions of great minds on life and ways of living it? I realize, of course, that there is danger in the alternative presentation; it may perhaps lead to sheer talk, to a superficial knowledge of an author. However, a wise teacher should be able to avoid these pitfalls.

If therefore we are really convinced of the importance of the humanities, that they should not only be a part of education but the very heart of it, we must combat its foes, external and internal. Indeed, if we were able to fight them successfully, we should make our education more than a road to a particular profession, more than a path to higher monetary returns, but a route to nobler living.

At the same time I wonder if those who have chosen to teach the humanities, are sufficiently devoted to them—if we really believe in them with all our souls. How widely are we accustomed to read in the literature which we are teaching? How extensively do we read in other literature? We cannot inspire unless we ourselves are inspired. Are we perhaps dispirited by the lack of support which we receive? Are we overwhelmed by our scientific colleagues and are tempted to imitate them? Do we regard factual material concerning our literature as more important than an understanding of the thoughts it conveys?

When all is said and done, the need is that we secure as teachers those who, in Cicero's words, are "all afire with these studies" (his *studiis flagrantis*). Assuredly nothing can catch fire unless a spark at least kindles it. I know of no automatic way of creating such a spark in teachers; it is a God-given gift. But in general to inspire such a teacher requires that fire shall have been transmitted from his teacher. Indeed it resembles the carrying of the Olympic torch, each runner kindling the fire from the torch of his predecessor and bearing it on its way to its final goal.

If our people are not led to the humanities and taught their significance, what will be the effect on the production of great works of letters among us? In general, works of genius flourish when the soil is receptive. It is no accident that in ancient Greece such a galaxy of great writers appeared at one time. When a people deeply appreciate writings of distinction, there will be a stimulus to their production. To be sure a great soul will speak even in an era of darkness, but an impetus to great work in any field rests upon the attitude of society. It is no accident that now we live in an age of noteworthy inventions and scientific discoveries, but I wonder how many works of today will endure in music, art or letters.

In times of sorrow and tribulation where does one turn for help? Not to the best-sellers in the fiction of the day but to the majestic works of the past. They alone can enable one to realize better what such suffering means and give one comfort in the dark days in which one is living. But unless one habitually turns to the great figures, he will not find it easy to open those doors when the need arises. We all know that sorrow and pain will overtake us, indeed more and more as the years grow more numerous. This means that with each year, each decade we need all the more the solace of great literature. I do not speak of the Bible since it is filled with so much that helps at such times; it should come first whenever the clouds gather. But next stand the great masters of letters. They do not confine themselves to trivial matters but give us the thoughts of the world's noblest minds on such crises as inevitably overtake us.

Unless we devote ourselves to the great works of the past and such great works as may perchance appear in our time, shall we not cut ourselves off both from those of our generation and also the majestic works which time has striven to preserve for us? We treasure the edifices of the past, some to be sure because of their architectural beauty, others merely because of historical associations and antiquity. And yet the works of literature go back into the dim centuries long before such buildings were erected. These are after all but things of brick and stone, often beautiful but at times esteemed merely as relics of a long past age. The works of letters are the distillations of great minds and great souls; they do not appear in mutilated form or in restorations.

They are the very words uttered by those long gone from mortal life but as living and as true as when the writer jotted them down. It is our duty to keep them alive and not permit them to take their place beside the mummies of Egyptian kings. Nothing is really more alive than they, if we but see that they are not buried and forgotten.

Unless we inculcate a love of great works and stimulate our students to read them—voluntarily and not as something prescribed in the course—above all read them when school and college are far in the past—unless, I say, we accomplish this, we shall fail in our greatest responsibility and make our times the true Dark Ages, ignorant of the past, devoted to the temporal and heedless of the eternal.

There is a passage in Maeterlinck's *Blue Bird* which I love to quote. The dead grandparents say in effect to the children "We dead live again when you the living think of us—and only then."

So the great figures of letters from Aeschylus to Milton only live when we of this generation read them and think their thoughts. Otherwise what life have they? They are truly dead —sometimes called dead in language but really dead in that they are completely ignored and forgotten.

We have therefore both affirmative and negative steps to take —to do everything possible to encourage love of great literature and at the same time to fight against the transformation of our educational institutions into institutions which can only by a stretch of terms be called educational—which seek to win popular favor by teaching or claiming to teach primarily that which is useful, useful in the narrowest sense of the term.

May we play our part in striving to convert our institutions into truly educational centers!

Let us recall the words of Kipling in his poem *The Secret of the Machines*. He represents the machines as boasting:

> We can pull and haul and push and lift and drive.
> We can print and plough and weave and heat and light,
> We can run and jump and swim and fly and dive,
> We can see and hear and count and read and write!

But later they are driven to admit:

> Our touch can alter all created things,
> We are everything on earth—except the Gods!

And finally they go even further and declare:

> Though our smoke may hide the Heavens from your eyes
> It will vanish and the stars will shine again,
> Because, for all our power and weight and size,
> We are nothing more than children of your brain!

So my plea in simplest terms is: "Let not the smoke of the world hide the heavens from our eyes."

ETHICAL AND RELIGIOUS IDEALS

MAKING LIFE WORTH LIVING [1]

JOHN SUTHERLAND BONNELL [2]

Dr. John Sutherland Bonnell gave this radio sermon on Sunday, January 4, 1953, over the American Broadcasting Company network. The address was the first in the 1953 National Vespers program, sponsored by the Broadcasting and Film Commission of the National Council of the Churches of Christ in the United States of America, and by the American Broadcasting Company.

Dr. Bonnell has been pastor of the Fifth Avenue Presbyterian Church since 1935. His homiletic ability and pulpit eloquence have attracted large audiences, as have his radio sermons.

His sermonic method is traditional. Although the speaker here uses no text, he quotes extensively from the Bible, organizes his material fully and simply, and incorporates many literary and other illustrations to attract and hold his "mass" audience.

His theology is conservative. But he is at all points interested in his direct counsel to his listeners rather than in dogma. He refuses to allow secular problems and ideas to dominate his message. (This talk has no reference to the events of the day.) He has strong personal leadership in the pulpit, and an excellent voice. During the past years he has grown steadily in pulpit leadership and influence in the United States.[3]

In the year 1883 a book was published in Scotland which brought to its author world-wide fame at the age of thirty-one. I refer to *Natural Law in the Spiritual World* by Henry Drummond. In it he sought to reconcile evangelical Christianity with the teachings of science.

This afternoon we are concerned only with one chapter of that book in which the author attempts to define life. He wrote

---

[1] Text supplied by the Broadcasting and Film Commission of the National Council of Churches of Christ in the United States of America, and reprinted by permission of Dr. John Sutherland Bonnell and the American Broadcasting Company.

[2] For biographical note, see Appendix.

[3] Cf. Bonnell's "Glory and Tragedy of Man," in *Representative American Speeches: 1946-1947*, p239-45. Consult also the sermons in the same volume by Fulton J. Sheen and Ralph W. Sockman.

that life is "correspondence with environment," borrowing his definition from Herbert Spencer, the biologist.

If we go back to a primitive animal organism, like the amoeba, which may be found in a stagnant pool, we discover a creature so low in the scale of life that it has no distinct organs whatsoever. It is little more than a sac of transparent structureless jelly. Says Drummond: "It corresponds with the smallest possible area of environment."

When we pass, however, from the amoeba to an insect the area of environment is greatly widened. Then we ascend the scale of life to man, where we see a remarkable happening. Man in his correspondence with his environment passes beyond the physical, which he transcends, and reaches out to the spiritual. This fact differentiates man from all the rest of creation.

Now, the successful continuation of life depends on whether or not the organism can remain in correspondence with its environment. Here, for instance, is a medusa, a form of jelly-fish. The restless waves of the ocean heave it far upon the rocks. The medusa, thrown into contact with a new environment with which it is unable to establish any correspondence, pays the forfeit with its life.

This is true of all forms of existence, including man. But man, with his spiritual endowments, establishes a correspondence with that eternal reality which is God.

It is important to note that when Jesus utters this statement: "I am come that they might have life, and that they might have it more abundantly," the evangelist in translating the sentence chooses one of two possible Greek words for 'life." He uses a word which, in the New Testament, signifies not a mere extension of time, but which carries with it profound moral and spiritual significance. It implies a capacity for nobler living.

"I am come that they might have life, and that they might have it more abundantly."

It is no prosaic or pedestrian existence that Christ offers to man, but a victorious and enduring life, which maintains a correspondence, not merely with the physical or material, the here and the now, but reaches out to correspond with the environment of eternity.

All normal human beings seek after life. So Tennyson sings:

> 'Tis life of which our nerves are scant
> 'Tis life, not death for which we pant,
> More life and fuller that we want.

Nevertheless, it is not the many but the few who achieve a full, rich, creative life. We are all too easily satisfied with life's second best. It was said of Goethe, the German philosopher, that he used to enjoy drawing in his spare time, but chose as the medium on which he drew grimy paper rather than white, lest his poor efforts would look too ridiculous.

So, when the challenge of Christ comes to men and women to leave the low levels of their past achievements and to dare the heights, they avert their eyes and sink back into a cheap and easy content.

No one of us has achieved more than the merest fraction of his capacity for living a full, rich, satisfying life. There are successive strata of undeveloped faculties within our souls, and Christ is ever summoning us to the highest.

Voltaire on one occasion said: "Most men die without having lived."

But the highest life of all for man is that in which he rises above the level of the beasts that perish; the life that corresponds with a spiritual environment. It was in this environment that Jesus constantly lived and worked. While He walked and talked with men, and ministered unto their infirmities, always around Him there were windows opening out to the Infinite. Into that life He ever seeks to lift us.

Have you ever thought of the amazing transformation He wrought upon His disciples—these fishermen, tax-gatherers, peasants, who possessed more than the average of human frailties? Under the spell of Christ they grew into spiritual giants who have become the inspiration of the ages.

Likewise, it is beyond our power to estimate the heightening of life that would be accomplished in each of us if we would only let Christ have His way. Then you could go back to that stubborn personal problem that defeated you, or to that domestic discord that has all but wrecked the happiness of your home, or to that profound difficulty which towers athwart your pathway like an impassable barrier, and by the power of Christ within you you should win a shining success at the very point of former defeat and failure.

An Old Testament prophet records a parallel happening wherein God so inspired an ordinary individual that he triumphed in the face of seemingly insuperable difficulties. Says the prophet: "This is the word of the Lord unto Zerubbabel, saying, Not by might, nor by power, but by my Spirit, saith the Lord of hosts. Who art thou, O great mountain? Before Zerubbabel thou shalt become a plain."

Now you see what Jesus meant when He says that if we have faith so much as a grain of mustard seed we shall say to a towering difficulty which looms before us like a mountain, "Get out of my way," and it will obey us. This is not wishful thinking; it is a verifiable fact.

I have seen in my ministry this oft-repeated miracle whereby Christ lays hold of discouraged human lives and molds and fashions them into courageous, resolute, consecrated personalities so that almost every semblance of their former disheartened selves has disappeared.

Another result of entering into the abundant life that Christ offers us is that our daily tasks take on new meaning and worthfulness. It is appalling how many people find their life work a deadly grind, monotonous and irksome. For others it is just a means of livelihood, a way to "get by." All this underscores the importance of a spiritual conception of one's vocation.

William Ewart Gladstone is one of history's most outstanding examples of a man who lived to serve his fellow men. Four times he was Prime Minister of Great Britain, and for sixty-one years he was a member of the British House of Commons. One day Mrs. Gladstone said to him: "I can't understand how you are able to bear up under the burdens of your office and of these savage and cruel attacks that are sometimes made on you by your political opponents."

He replied quietly: "It is only because I try to live *sub specie aeternitatis*"—under the form of eternity! He let something of the light of heaven fall upon his daily tasks.

What a transformation would come over our workaday world if the teacher in the classroom, the carpenter at his bench, the painter with his brush, the merchant behind the counter, the banker at his desk, the housewife in the home, the doctor in his clinic and the minister in his study were each and all to pause in the morning at the threshold of their labors and say: "What I do here today I shall do for the glory of God, and may His blessing rest upon it." Then an unwonted radiance would invest all human toil, and we should know something of the glory of God's kingdom on earth.

Finally, we shall discover the abundant life as we lose ourselves in a cause greater than our little lives.

F. B. Sanborn, in his recollections of Thoreau, says that the Thoreau family gave themselves with such complete devotion to the liberation of the slaves that every member of it possessed an elevation of character which imparted an air of dignity to the trivial details of life.

Whenever we give ourselves to some noble crusade it does just that for us. Have you ever thought, for instance, that there has not been in history a great orator who has deeply moved the hearts of men, who was not himself inspired by some great cause into which he had flung himself with abandon? There was Demosthenes, rousing the people of Athens against Philip of Macedonia; Cicero, with his eloquent attacks upon Catiline and other enemies of the Roman Republic who were traitors; Patrick Henry, in his rousing challenge to the foes of American liberty; Daniel Webster, pleading for the maintenance of the American Union; Daniel O'Connell, with his crusade for Irish independence; John Bright, denouncing the evils of the Crimean War, and setting forth in alluring terms his vision of universal peace; and Winston Churchill, standing upon the embattled Isle of Britain and hurling defiance in the face of the tyrant aggressor. Not one of these men could have risen to half his stature had it not been for the cause into which he flung his life.

It is not otherwise with the prophets of God. See them standing in serried ranks, these eloquent advocates of the merits of their Redeemer: St. Paul, St. Ambrose, St. Francis, Savonarola, Luther, Knox, Chalmers, Wesley, Whitefield, Phillips Brooks, Henry Ward Beecher, and a host of others who so exalted their crucified but risen Lord that all men were drawn to Him.

Have you a cause to which you give yourself—a cause that calls for the noblest and best within you? The cause of Christ's Church and Kingdom inspired these men. Will you "follow in their train?" Never in history was the message of the Church needed more than today. Amid all the confusion and bewilderment of our time the Church of Jesus Christ stands strong, immovable, bearing calm witness to the sovereignty of Eternal God, and calling men and women back to the acknowledgment of His divine will in human affairs. The Church militant is facing desperate and implacable foes. She is not on dress parade; she is girded for conflict. Wherever there is anyone who believes that Christ has the answer for human problems, that person ought to be within the Christian Church. When we stand alone fronting the evils of the world our courage oozes away, and heart and strength faint and fail.

No believer can be truly strong until he has taken his place in the ranks of the Christian Church, and has felt the comradeship of the Cross. There the influence of each individual is multiplied a thousandfold. Are you one of that glorious company? If not, why shouldn't you answer the call of Christ today?

PRAYER:

Eternal God, forgive us that we have lived amid life's shallows when Thou hast meant us to launch out into the deep; that we have used only a fraction of the powers Thou has entrusted to us; that so long we have been far less than our best.

O Thou Shepherd of the souls of men, lead us into life more abundant for until we live like this we have never lived at all.

In the name of Christ. Amen.

THERE LIES OUR FRONTIER [4]

ALEXANDER WINSTON [5]

Dr. Alexander Winston gave this address at a Lenten service in the Immanuel Church, Portland, Maine, on March 17, 1953.

The sermon is an excellent example of homiletic organization, with introduction, statement of thesis (but with no Biblical text), well articulated series of main points, and concluding summary and appeal. Each topic is developed within the framework of the speaker's theological concepts, yet with sufficient illustration, including historical reference, to clarify and illumine each step of development.

The point of view is that of "liberal conservatism." The speaker has attempted to invest ancient Christian concepts with contemporary meaning and application. Dr. Winston has a degree in philosophy from Washington State University, and has had advanced studies at Meadville and at University of Chicago theological seminaries (with a B.D. degree), also at the universities of Paris and Marburg. In this sermon severe scholarship, although apparent, is carefully controlled to meet the needs of the average layman. The language is unhackneyed.

According to Dr. Winston, "Great preaching must fulfill a double demand: (1) convey the truth; (2) do so in memorable and compelling language. The first demand is satisfied only by a rigorous use of all the tools of the mind: sensitive perception, reason, and a healthy respect for a fact. The second demand requires art rather than logic." [6] Such philosophy of speaking is Aristotelian, but is sound doctrine for effective speakers of all kinds today.

To pioneer is the peculiar treasure of America. While, for two centuries, we were thrusting our geographical frontiers over plain and mountain to the salt shore of the western sea, the spiritual leaders of America were making their frontier advances in the realm of religious thought. Their rallying-cry was the stirring admonition of old John Robinson to the Pilgrims at Leyden: "The Lord hath more truth and light yet to break forth out of His holy word." Our fathers ardently sought how they could deepen and expand the divine light which was their inheritance.

[4] Text supplied by Dr. Alexander Winston with the courtesy of this reprinting.
[5] For biographical note, see Appendix.
[6] Letter to this editor, February 3, 1953.

As a result, it is a solid conviction among us that every religious movement must keep pressing forward, purifying what it is and ennobling what it seeks to be. To stand still is to retreat; to retreat is to perish. We perceive this hour to be an authentic hour of advance, marked by the opening of avenues into an untried but commanding future, whose summons is too imperative to be ignored. Our problem is not whether we shall move into that future at all; rather we must at this juncture in our history ask *how* we shall advance and *what* future shall environ us.

The thesis of this sermon may be stated simply as follows: *We shall substantially advance when, and only when, we bear witness in our own lives to the full power and import of pure Christianity.* This we have not as yet done. Pure Christianity offers us an ample spiritual frontier, a gospel for the sorry world's salvation, and a moral blueprint for the comonwealth of righteousness among men. It is for us to make that gospel flesh.

There is a natural temptation, in troublous times, when the soul is shaken with uncertainty, to take the easy path toward a bizarre and rootless faith. Yet to flee from the Christian concept of God and man is to emulate the benighted individual who hurries from continent to continent bent on escaping his own soul. We cannot escape our souls by hectic flights toward some novel ecclesiastical vantage point. On the contrary, we can fulfill our soul's high promise only by a new and flaming devotion to the simple Christian teachings that have invigorated every age of faith. Tomorrow's task is to make our lives a persuasive testimony to the whole piety, social vision, moral responsibility and brotherly love enjoined by the historic faith which our fathers tested in the glowing fire of their times. More than any new principle, we sorely need the fearless and unequivocal application of principles now in our possession. These principles are universal in application, basic to the needs of life, and as perennially modern as are the truths of mathematics. But they can no longer simply be talked about. The president of Mt. Holyoke College once said to her students: "Love God, and do something about it!" Out of such advice can our future be made, for our effectiveness lies in ordering our lives, with a fresh intensity, according to the great realities of pure Christianity. Those realities are five in number.

First, *our faith will advance when we are a living testimony to the reality of God*. To the profoundest liberal Christianity, God is sovereign Creator of all that is, loving Father of our spirits, and righteous Judge over our lives. As Creator, He set the whirling constellations in the flight, rounded the blue dome of heaven, raised the sky for a parapet and laid the moon thereon, locked up the salt seas within the shores and ordered the channels of the deep. Moreover, as Creator He has been the continuing source of growth and development in the upward journey of living things from the black muck of a steaming antediluvian swamp to the resplendent glory of man's genius.

Let us ask ourselves why that upward journey has taken place and continues even until now. It is one of three things: either by chance or by fate or by a personal will. Was it by chance? Not only is this answer a dagger-stroke at any humane philosophy of life; it is irrational as well, for the possibility of a coherent world evolving by sheer chance is so small as to be absurd. Was it then fate? If so, all meaning is lost from what men do, and we are playing out a poor shabby drama without freedom, without hope and without understanding. If it is not chance or fate that impels the evolutionary process, there is but one alternative left: *purpose,* and a cosmic purpose can be had only by a cosmic personal will. Our world possesses meaning and can possess meaning only because its Creator is God, who through His personal will establishes and unfolds the main lines of history. Within those lines we, as free men, make our decisions and play our part.

Yet God is more than creative will. In Christian teaching He is preeminently a loving Father, a near presence in Whom love and forgiveness are immediately known to the devoted servant of His will. Modern man, like the contemporaries of Jesus, is nourished by the assurance of God's loving care. An army chaplain reports that the Bible in the library of his hospital ship was most worn from use at the 139th Psalm: "If I ascend up into heaven, thou art there; if I make my bed in the grave, behold thou art there." No one would accuse those soldiers of cowardly fear. They have outfaced death in the green hell of the South Pacific, and many of them would not shrink from facing death again. Yet they find it natural, healthy and sane to look for guidance from their heavenly Father.

Furthermore, we have learned in the bitterness of the last three decades that God is also a God of judgment. His creation is undergirded by strict moral law, and He returns to men whirlwinds for the winds that men blithely sow. Alexis Carrel tells the story of a French peasant who sat alone after the church service had finished, and who, when asked why he remained in his seat, replied: "I am looking at God and He is looking at me." So! in these days we know the impact of a judgment as immediate as that. Thus for the profoundest liberal Christianity, God is all that I have named: sovereign Creator of the world, loving Father of our spirit, and righteous Judge over our lives.

Secondly, *the service of man, which is integral to our faith, depends upon our ability to see human nature realistically,* not make of man a dusty worm in the dour tradition of Calvinism, nor endow him with the attributes of a potential perfection, as sentimental liberalism has done. Man is a child of God, created in His image, full of promise and wondrously made. He has immense powers of thought and imagination, and an astonishing capacity for courageous devotion. As such, it may well be said that the spirit of man is the candle of the Lord.

However, to stop here in the description of man's nature is to give an unrealistic and incomplete account of him, an account which cannot possibly work out for his good because it is not a true reporting of his real nature. Man's spirit, granted to be the candle of the Lord, is often a candle wavering and uncertain, forever in need of God's own grace and mercy to add vigor to its flame. Men can be evil, selfish, cruel, lustful, proud, greedy and cynical, as well as good, loving, chaste, humble, devoted, faithful. All of us can testify to the truth of Paul's cry: "What I would, that do I not: but what I hate, that do I."

In brief, the essence of man's freedom is his real opportunity to choose evil as well as good, an opportunity which can neither be a shadow nor a sham, and which validates itself in the fact that the evil choice is often made. Whether the choice be good or ill, the church has its religious role to play. If a man chooses the good, and the commandments of God are followed, he knows the fulfillment of life, its elevation and moral grandeur, and that "peace at the center" of his being which is a jewel without price. If he makes an evil choice, freighted with demonic passion, there follows a need for confession, mercy and forgiveness, a reckoning with the austere relentlessness of the moral law, and instruction in the strait way of righteousness. But for Christianity to serve man properly, it must view him realistically as he in fact is: wonderfully potential for good, terribly potential for ill. To the Church, man is less an achievement than an opportunity.

Third, *our faith will advance when we are a living testimony to the spirit that was in Jesus.* John Middleton Murry, the eminent literary critic, and a man of skeptical mind, once said: "The time has come when I must make up my mind about Jesus." That time has come for us all. However diverse may be our interpretations of Jesus' character, of one thing we are sure: his life was sufficient for the founding of a faith. To his many-sided character the disciples responded with the fervor of men who had found life's hope and meaning. "As many as received him," says the Fourth Gospel, "to them gave he power." To them he revealed the nature of God with an undeniable immediacy. He acted for them like a prism, breaking the white light ineffable of Deity into earthly colors for us to see—the colors of love, mercy, compassion, hope.

We discover today, as the disciples deeply discovered before us, that the longer we live with the words and deeds of Jesus of Nazareth, the more valid they become. Consider how you would test a coin. First, you toss it on a marble counter and listen for the ring of the true metal, then you carry it to an assayer who can analyze its elements, and finally you present it to the Treasury of the United States for validation. So with Jesus of Nazareth: we absorb the story of his life unthinkingly as part of our Christian civilization. Later we test his teachings in the crucible of our own soul-shaking experiences, or we may subject them to the passionless scrutiny of modern scholarship. Then, in moments of profoundest insight, when we supremely see the nature of reality, and realize our fullest manhood in the richness of communion with God, the leadership of Jesus receives final validation. He meets the test: he is the true coin; he is approved in the sober judgment of our best and wisest mind.

As much as Jesus of Nazareth means to liberal Christianity, the idea of Christ is even closer to our free-church tradition. By Jesus we mean the man who lived in a certain place and at a certain time of history, and whose human activities are to be circumscribed by the hours of birth and death. He was born, lived, died and was buried. The idea of Christ knows no such limitations. It is more universal, more akin to the priesthood of all believers and the salavation of all pure souls. It is the unfolding of the original life and teaching; the exfoliation of the seed planted by the prophet of prophets; the expansion and proliferation of the simple gospel preached in the Galilean streets and hills.

When we think of the spirit of Christ, we think of a thousand unknown saints and apostles to whom to be called Christian was the highest honor. We think of the little poor man of Assisi, preaching to the birds and building his church with his own hands. We think of Luther at the Diet of Worms, crying out with the voice of the whole Reformation: "Here I stand. I cannot do otherwise. So help me God." We think of the dim glory of European cathedrals; of the smallest and poorest mission in the wilds of some frontier land; of chaplains setting up altars on the radiators of jeeps under hostile fire. We think of John Wesley preaching on the hillside to Cornish colliers until the tears made furrows through the grime of their cheeks. We think of Norwegians standing in the snow outside their churches singing "A Mighty Fortress is Our God," while the soldiers of occupation seized pulpit and pastor. We think of the all-night service on Christmas Eve at the ancient church in Bethlehem of Judea; of shop-preachers toiling at the lathe by day and preaching in store-fronts of Detroit at night. Of all these we think and many more, because all are in the spirit of Christ. His was the mustard seed which grew until the birds of heaven might come and sing in the branches thereof.

The whole fact can be stated thus: in the life of Jesus something got abroad in the world. Men may differ about the exact nature of that "something," and differ they most certainly do.

Yet they continue to agree that the "something" is the best clue we have to the world's salvation, and that the "something" can be most practicably described as "the spirit of Christ."

Fourth, *our faith will advance when we are a living testimony to the reality of the organic, historic church.* A church is a living thing, as truly organic as the people who belong to it. It is born, matures, adjusts itself to environment, or, if unsuccessful in meeting the demands of its environment, it dies. Liberal Christians have erroneously believed that they could create, order and destroy institutions at will, by the simple application of reasoned thinking. We have talked about "rational religion" as though the spiritual life were primarily a matter of logic, and we have worked on the tacit assumption that if a religious idea could not be proved by science or reason, we would be either fools or cowards to believe that idea. Such thinking delivered liberal Christianity into a pit of skepticism from whence, considerably chastened, it now begins to see its errors.

For one thing we see that it is difficult, if not impossible, to prove (either by science or logic) anything important about religion. There is no accepted proof for the existence of God, for our own souls, for free-will, or for immortality. Furthermore there is no accepted proof for any of our ethical ideas, moral convictions, or esthetic tastes. Indeed, we cannot rationally prove that the world was really here yesterday or that it will be here tomorrow. In fact, science and logic themselves are possible only if there are admitted to be some things which cannot be proved and must be taken on faith.

Liberal Christianity sees now that we have been very busy disinfecting our religious practices of every trace of what science might call superstition, and now we find that we cannot live on disinfectant. Just as it is possible to prune a tree with a knife, but it is not possible to grow a tree with a knife, so it is possible (and good) to criticize religion by the methods of science and reason, but it is impossible to create and sustain an abiding faith by those means.

The church is a living organism. If you cut it, it will bleed; if you sever its roots, it will die. A tree which does not take the natural form derived from its seed is monstrous and unhealthy.

Our seed is the life and teachings of Jesus, and there is a sanely healthy form given to our growth by that irreducible fact of history. Only such an institution, made of the stuff of humanity, and remaining true to its organic growth, can endure. Only such a church can go anywhere except into oblivion.

Europe learned its lesson in the hard terms of liberal collapse. Unfortified by a sturdy gospel, rootless and ephemeral, the liberal churches of Europe vanished or capitulated before the fierce flood of competing ideologies. See Friedrich Heiler, a great German theologian, restricted to teaching Hindu mysticism to his classes in Marburg University, trying to make his voice heard above the crashing of soldiers' boots upon the cobble-stones outside his classroom. To watch his unsounding lips, as I have done, would be poignantly to know the fate of liberal churches on Europe's shattered continent. Their lips, too, are soundless; instead it is the Reformation churches who have maintained Christian teachings and practice against every threat. To them the church is a living thing, the faith of their fathers and their fathers' fathers, the token of eternity made flesh. They rise up like Luther before them, saying: "Here we stand. We cannot do otherwise. So help us God."

Fifth, *our faith will advance when we are a living testimony to the reality of human brotherhood.* It is essential that our church begin now to apply the idea of brotherhood in public affairs with a determination heretofore unknown among us. Our whole social gospel stems from this one concept.

We must earnestly seek brotherhood between the nations. Upon no other basis can an enduring peace be built. Treaties are but scraps of paper, international organizations are a hollow mockery breeding disillusionment, if the foundation is not a minimum of brotherhood. It is imperative that there gather now a unified Christian opinion, reaffirming the ancient truth that balances of power are a snare and a deceit. Unless the Lord build a city it cannot be built. Coalitions of world powers that look impregnable today will dissolve tomorrow under utterly unpredictable conditions. The cement of international peace is an adequate sense of a shared world. "Not by might, not by strength, not by power, but by my spirit, saith the Lord."

In addition, the church of tomorrow must stand for brother-hood of men on the economic level. The economic man is haunted by the modern paradox of abundant production and abundant need which he seems unable to bring together. The family ideal, upon which Christian ethics is erected, is largely repudiated in the practice of commerce. The family does not need a deadly competitive warfare between its members in order to maintain the family economy, yet society at large continues to preserve such a lethal system and to exalt it. We all see how foreign the concept of brotherhood is to a deliberately internecine struggle. In seeking a way out of our predicament it is well to remember that the solution does not lie with any one economic class. Manager and laborer, producer and consumer are all human beings, capable of mistakes, spurred by self-interest and eager for power. Therefore, the task of the church is primarily moral: to inculcate in all members of our economic order a sense of community, or mutual responsibility.

Finally, it is essential that brotherhood between races be brought from the realm of felicitous phrases and be concretely applied. No reputable sociologist or anthropologist finds any significant difference between the races of the world. The slight variations of facial characteristics and color are far out-weighted by essential similarities. In blood, intelligence and emotional reaction there is a general parity. Tomorrow's world, with the emergence of new and unpredictable racial groupings, will ignore the equality of races at its own peril. To do so is more than un-Christian; it is impracticable. How shall we live successfully with Russia, South America, Japan, China, India, and the Mediterranean crescent of Arabs, if we persist in considering some or all of those people racially inferior? Mankind is crying out in agony at this breach of fundamental Christian social ethics. The solution dies deeper than congressional acts or other external adjustments, important as these are. The hearts of men must change—take out their hearts of stone and put in hearts of flesh—if we are ever to be a united world. "Not by might, not by strength, not by power, but by my spirit, saith the Lord."

These are the five realities toward which a sound Christian advance can be launched. We are in the valley of decision. The urgency of the times has sharpened the issue for us. Shall we or shall we not derive our sustenance from pure Christianity, as we confront a world heavy with sweat, drenched in blood, surfeited with tears? The choice is sharp and clean. Remember how Pizarro stood before his travel-weary and emaciated band of men upon the shore of what is now Colombia, and drew upon the sand a line with his rapier. "Those who wish for ease and security," he said, "may return. As for me, I go south." So stand we. In many directions lies ease and security; in some directions lie bizarre and shallow philosophies. Ahead is the way of pure Christianity, adequate to the earth's salvation, of universal import, and eternally modern. It is a strait way, a severe trial for flabby minds or unstable temperaments. It is a broad way, unmarked throughout vast stretches of its course. There lies our frontier. Let us resolve to take that road, as we are earnestly charged in conscience by the Lord our God, until His true church shall come into its own.

APPENDIX

BIOGRAPHICAL NOTES

BARKLEY, ALBEN WILLIAM (1877-   ). Born in Graves County, Kentucky; A.B., Marvin College, Kentucky, 1897; studied at Emory College, and at the University of Virginia Law School; practiced law since 1901; member of the Sixty-third to the Sixty-ninth Congresses, 1913-1927; United States Senator 1927-49; reelected Senator in 1939 after a strenuous primary campaign against A. B. Chandler, of Kentucky; Senate leader of the Administration party, 1937-1948, resigned on February 24, 1944, and was unanimously reelected to that position; Vice President of the United States, 1948-1952. (See also *Current Biography: 1949.*)

BONNELL, JOHN SUTHERLAND (1893-   ). Born in Prince Edward Island, Canada; A.B., Dalhousie University, 1919; B.D., Pine Hill Divinity School, Halifax, 1927, D.D., 1934; LL.D., Washington and Jefferson, 1943; pastor of Canadian churches, 1922-35; pastor of Fifth Avenue Presbyterian Church, New York City, since 1935; lecturer, Union Theological Seminary, Princeton Theological Seminary, since 1938; preacher in England, Scotland, 1941; served in Canadian Army, World War I, 1916-18; member, Sigma Xi; author of *Fifth Avenue Sermons,* 1936; *Pastoral Psychiatry,* 1938; *Britons Under Fire,* 1941; and later volumes of sermons; weekly broadcast over the American Broadcasting Company network. (See also *Current Biography: 1945.*)

BRADLEY, OMAR NELSON (1893-   ). Born, Clark, Missouri; B.S., United States Military Academy, 1915; Command and General Staff School, 1929; Army War College, 1934; honorary LL.D., University of Missouri, Drury College, Harvard, Dartmouth, Princeton, and many other colleges and universities; commander, 2nd lieutenant, infantry, U.S. Army, 1915, advanced through the grades to general, 1915-45; in campaigns in Tunis, Sicily, Normandy, France, Germany, 1944-45; administrator, veterans' affairs, 1945-47; chief of Staff of U.S. Army, 1948-49; chairman, Army-Navy-Air Force Joint Chiefs of Staff, 1949-53; awarded many military honors and decorations. (See also *Current Biography: 1943*.)

DEUTSCH, MONROE EMANUEL (1879-   ). Born in San Francisco; A.B., University of California, 1902, A.M., 1903, Ph.D., 1911; LL.D., St. Mary's College, 1933, and various other colleges; instructor, assistant professor, professor of Greek and Latin, from 1907 until his retirement, 1947, University of California; dean of the College of Letters and Science, 1922-30, vice president and provost, 1931-47; officer in many philanthropic and learned societies; member, Phi Beta Kappa; author of *Our Legacy of Religious Freedom*, 1941; *The Letter and the Spirit*, 1943.

DULLES, JOHN FOSTER (1888-   ). Born in Washington, D.C.; B.A., Princeton, 1908, LL.D., 1946; Sorbonne, Paris, 1908-09; LL.B., George Washington University, 1911; LL.D., Tufts, Wagner, Northwestern; began law practice, New York City, 1911; director, Bank of New York; trustee, Rockefeller Foundation; chairman, Carnegie Endowment for International Peace; chairman, Federal Council of Churches Commission on a Just and Durable Peace; secretary, Hague Peace Conference, 1907; captain and major, U.S. Army, 1917-18; member, Reparations Commission and Supreme Economic Council, 1919; member, United States delegation, San Francisco Conference on World Organization, 1945; Council of Foreign Ministers, London, 1945; General Assembly, United Nations, 1946; meeting of Council of Foreign Ministers, Moscow, 1947; London meeting of "Big Four," 1947; U.S. Senator from New York, July-November 1949 (to complete term of Senator Wagner); appointed counsellor, Department of State, April 1950; appointed, with rank of Ambassador to negotiate terms of peace for Japan, 1951; representative at signing of Japanese Peace Treaty, San Francisco, 1951; writer and speaker on international affairs;

War or Peace, 1950; appointed Secretary of State in the Eisenhower Administration, 1953. (See also *Current Biography: 1949.*)

EASTVOLD, DONALD W. E. (1914-   ). Born in Minneapolis; attended schools at Eau Claire, Wisconsin; at eighteen, made speeches for Republican senatorial candidate; United States Army, 1942-46; University of Minnesota Law School, 1946-48; LL.B., University of Washington Law School, 1948; prosecuting attorney, Pierce County, Washington; elected to the Washington State Senate, 1950; elected Attorney General, State of Washington, November 1952.

EISENHOWER, DWIGHT D. (1890-   ). Born in Denison, Texas; B.S., United States Military Academy, 1915; Army Tank School, 1921; graduate, War College, 1929; 2nd Lieutenant, U.S. Army, 1915; Lieutenant Colonel, Tank Corps, World War I; advanced through grades to General of the Army, December 1944; Chief of Operations Division, Office of Chief of Staff, 1942; Commanding General, European Theatre of Operations, June 1942; Allied Commander in Chief, North Africa, November 1942; Supreme Commander of Allied Land, Sea, and Air Forces in Western Europe, November 1943; Chief of Staff, U.S. Army, 1945-48; elected President of Columbia University, 1948; appointed Supreme Commander of the North Atlantic Treaty Nations, 1950; entered in presidential primaries on Republican ticket, January 1952; author of *Crusade in Europe,* 1948, *Eisenhower Speaks,* 1948; elected President of the United States, November 1952. (See also *Current Biography: 1948.*)

FORD, HENRY II (1917-   ). Born, Detroit, Michigan; grandson of Henry Ford; attended Detroit University School; graduate of Hotchkiss School, 1936; at Yale, 1936-40; with Ford Motor Company after 1941; president since 1945; lieutenant (j.g.), U.S. Navy, 1941, released to direct war production of Ford Motor Company, 1943; recipient of Thomas A. Edison Award, 1947; member, Advisory Council, Department of Commerce; member of board of trustees, Committee for Economic Development. (See also *Current Biography: 1946.*)

HAND, LEARNED (1872-   ). Born, Albany, New York; A.B. Harvard, 1893, A.M., 1894; LL.B., Harvard Law School, 1896; LL.D., Columbia, 1930, and degrees from other representative institutions since, including one from the University of the State of New York, 1953; admitted to the bar, 1897; practised law, Albany and New York City, 1897-1909; U.S. District Judge, Southern District of New York, 1909-1924; U.S. Judge, Second District, since 1924; contributor to various legal publications; his legal opinions widely recognized as superior in thought and expression.   (See also *Current Biography: 1950*.)

HOLLAND, SPESSARD LINDSEY (1892-   ). Born at Bartow, Florida; PH.B. (magna cum laude), Emory College, 1912, LL.D., 1943; LL.B., University of Florida, 1916; LL.D., Rollins College, 1941; teacher, secondary schools, 1912-14; teacher, University of Florida, preparatory department, 1914-16; practice of law at Bartow since 1916; county judge, 1921-29; Florida State Senator, 1932-40; governor of Florida, 1941-45; United States Senator since 1946; World War I, service (promoted to captaincy), Distinguished Service Cross, 1918; member of numerous public service boards; Phi Kappa Phi, Phi Beta Kappa.   (See also *Current Biography: 1950*.)

KIRK, GRAYSON (1903-   ). Born, Jeffersonville, Ohio; A.B., Miami (O.), 1924, Phi Beta Kappa, cum laude; M.A., Clark, 1925; teacher, secondary school, now LaMar College, Beaumont, Texas, 1925-27; Ph.D., in political science, University of Wisconsin, 1930; teacher, political science, Wisconsin, 1930-38; promoted successively to full professor; studied at the London School of Economics, 1938-39; associate professor of government at Columbia, 1940-43, professor of government, 1943; professor of international relations, 1947-49; provost, 1949-52, and president since January 1953. Wartime activities included service in the State Department, 1942. (See also *Current Biography: 1951.)*

LEHMAN, HERBERT H. (1878-   ). Born in New York City; B.A., Williams, 1899, M.A., 1921, LL. D., 1929; honorary degrees, Yeshiva, New York University, Hamilton, Syracuse, Fordham, and other institutions; partner in Lehman Brothers, bankers, 1908; elected lieutenant-governor, New York State, 1928, reelected, 1930; governor, 1932-42; appointed director of foreign relief and rehabilitation operations, Department of State, 1942; director general United Nations Relief and Rehabilitation Administration, 1943-46; member ECA board for European aid, 1948; captain in U.S. Army, 1917-19, promoted to Colonel, General Staff; awarded D.S.M., 1919; decorated by many foreign countries for service to humanity; trustee or director of many charitable organizations; appointed U.S. Senator, 1949; elected for six-year term, 1951.

LODGE, HENRY CABOT, JR. (1902-   ). Born, Nahant, Massachusetts; grandson of the late Senator Henry Cabot Lodge; A.B., Harvard, 1924; with the Boston *Evening Transcript,* 1923; New York *Herald Tribune,* 1924; member of the Massachusetts General Court, 1933-36; elected to the United States Senate from Massachusetts, 1936, for term ending 1943; on leave, major in the U.S. Army Tank Corps, with British forces, 1942; lieutenant-colonel, southern France, Rhine, southern Germany, 1944-45; reelected to Senate, 1946; defeated for reelection, 1952; appointed by President Eisenhower, United States chief delegate to the United Nations, 1953. (See also *Current Biography: 1943.*)

NIXON, RICHARD MILHOUS (1913-   ). Born at Yorba Linda, California; A.B., Whittier College, 1934; LL.B., Duke University Law School, 1937; general practice of law, Whittier, California, 1937-42; attorney with Office of Emergency Management, Washington, D.C., 1942; Lieutenant-Commander, U.S. Navy, 1942-46; member of 80th and 81st Congresses, 1947-51; elected Vice President of the United States on the Republican ticket, 1952. (See also *Current Biography: 1949.*)

STEVENSON, ADLAI E. (1900-   ). Born in Los Angeles, California; A.B., Princeton, 1922; J.D., Northwestern University Law School, 1926; LL.D., Illinois Wesleyan, Northwestern, Bradley; reporter, *Daily Pantograph* (Bloomington, Illinois),

1924-25; admitted to Illinois bar, 1926; member, Chicago, Illinois, law firms, 1927-41; assistant to Secretary of Navy, 1941-44; chief, Foreign Economic Administrations, 1943; assistant to Secretary of State, 1945; adviser, U.S. delegation General Assembly, United Nations; governor of Illinois, 1948-52; nominated for the presidency on the Democratic ticket; defeated in the election, November 1952; tour around the world, 1953. (See also *Current Biography: 1949.)*

SYMINGTON, WILLIAM STUART (1901-   ). Born, Amherst, Massachusetts; served in the United States Army, 1918; at Yale, 1919-23; International Correspondence School; with Symington Companies, Rochester, New York, 1923-35; Rustless Iron and Steel Company, Baltimore, Md., 1935-37; president, Emerson Electric Manufacturing Company, St. Louis, Mo., 1938-45; surplus property administrator, Washington, 1945-46; Assistant Secretary of War for Air, 1945-47; Secretary of Air Force, National Defense, 1947-50; chairman, National Security Resources Board, 1950; elected United States Senator from Missouri, 1952. (See also *Current Biography: 1945.*)

TRUMAN, HARRY S. (1894-   ). Born in Lamar, Missouri; student, Kansas City School of Law, 1923-25; captain, Field Artillery, World War I; judge, Jackson County Court, 1922-24; presiding judge, 1926-34; United States Senator from Missouri, 1935-41, reelected for the term 1941-47; elected Vice President of the United States on the Democratic ticket, November 1944; sworn in as President on the death of President Roosevelt, April 1945; elected President in 1948; refused candidacy for reelection and retired, January 1953. (See also *Current Biography: 1945.)*

WINSTON, ALEXANDER (1909-   ). Born, Seattle, Washington; attended Seattle public schools; A.B., University of Washington, 1930 (Phi Beta Kappa and *cum laude*); M.A., in literature, 1931; doctorate in philosophy, 1949; at Meadville Theological School and University of Chicago, B.D., 1935; awarded Cruft Fellowship, studied at the University of Paris and at Marburg; since 1936, has served pastorates in Seattle, Boston, and Portland, Maine; at the United Church on the Green, New Haven, after May 1953; since 1944, member of faculty at Tufts College; has published two volumes of sermons: *You are the Key* (1949), *I Leave You My Heart* (1951).

YOUNG, ROBERT RALPH (1897-   ). Born in Canadian, Texas; student, Culver Military Academy, 1912-14 (head of his class); University of Virginia, 1914-16; with Du Pont Company, 1916-20; with General Motors Corporation, 1922-29; partner, Young, Kolbe and Company (members, New York Stock Exchange), 1932-37; chairman of board, Chesapeake and Ohio Railway Company; cited by Forbes Magazine in 1947 as one of "today's fifty foremost business leaders"; author of monthly articles for *Railway Progress*; contributor to other magazines. (See also *Current Biography: 1947.*)

CUMULATIVE AUTHOR INDEX

An author index to the volumes of *Representative American Speeches* for the years 1937-1938 through 1952-1953. The date following the title of each speech indicates the volume in which it appears.